ACKNOWLEDGING
WRITING PARTNERS

PERSPECTIVES ON WRITING
Series Editors, Susan H. McLeod and Rich Rice

The Perspectives on Writing series addresses writing studies in a broad sense. Consistent with the wide ranging approaches characteristic of teaching and scholarship in writing across the curriculum, the series presents works that take divergent perspectives on working as a writer, teaching writing, administering writing programs, and studying writing in its various forms.

The WAC Clearinghouse, Colorado State University Open Press, and University Press of Colorado are collaborating so that these books will be widely available through free digital distribution and low-cost print editions. The publishers and the Series editors are committed to the principle that knowledge should freely circulate. We see the opportunities that new technologies have for further democratizing knowledge. And we see that to share the power of writing is to share the means for all to articulate their needs, interest, and learning into the great experiment of literacy.

Recent Books in the Series

Seth Kahn, William B. Lalicker, and Amy Lynch-Biniek (Eds.), *Contingency, Exploitation, and Solidarity: Labor and Action in English Composition* (2017)

Barbara J. D'Angelo, Sandra Jamieson, Barry Maid, and Janice R. Walker (Eds.), *Information Literacy: Research and Collaboration across Disciplines* (2017)

Justin Everett and Cristina Hanganu-Bresch (Eds.), *A Minefield of Dreams: Triumphs and Travails of Independent Writing Programs* (2016)

Chris M. Anson and Jessie L. Moore (Eds.), *Critical Transitions: Writing and the Questions of Transfer* (2016)

Joanne Addison and Sharon James McGee, *Writing and School Reform: Writing Instruction in the Age of Common Core and Standardized Testing* (2016)

Lisa Emerson, *The Forgotten Tribe: Scientists as Writers* (2016)

Jacob S. Blumner and Pamela B. Childers, *WAC Partnerships Between Secondary and Postsecondary Institutions* (2015)

Nathan Shepley, *Placing the History of College Writing: Stories from the Incomplete Archive* (2015)

Asao B. Inoue, *Antiracist Writing Assessment Ecologies: An Approach to Teaching and Assessing Writing for a Socially Just Future* (2015)

Theresa Lillis, Kathy Harrington, Mary R. Lea, and Sally Mitchell (Eds.), *Working with Academic Literacies: Case Studies Towards Transformative Practice* (2015)

ACKNOWLEDGING WRITING PARTNERS

By Laura R. Micciche

The WAC Clearinghouse
wac.colostate.edu
Fort Collins, Colorado

University Press of Colorado
upcolorado.com
Boulder, Colorado

The WAC Clearinghouse, Fort Collins, Colorado 80523–1040

University Press of Colorado, Boulder, Colorado 80303

Printed in the United States of America

Library of Congress Cataloging-in-Publication Data

Names: Micciche, Laura R., author.
Title: Acknowledging writing partners / by Laura R. Micciche.
Other titles: Perspectives on writing (Fort Collins, Colo.)
Description: Fort Collins : WAC Clearinghouse ; Boulder, Colorado : University Press of
   Colorado, [2017] | Series: Perspectives on writing | Includes bibliographical references and
   index.
Identifiers: LCCN 2017034927| ISBN 9781607327677 (pbk.) | ISBN 9781607327684 (ebook)
Subjects: LCSH: Authorship—Collaboration. | Authorship—Social aspects. | Paratext. |
   Academic writing. | Gratitude.
Classification: LCC PN145 .M4857 2017 | DDC 808.02—dc23
LC record available at https://lccn.loc.gov/2017034927

Copyeditor: Kenna Neitch
Designer: Mike Palmquist
Cover Photo: Jenn Fishman
Series Editors: Susan H. McLeod and Rich Rice

This book is printed on acid-free paper.

The WAC Clearinghouse supports teachers of writing across the disciplines. Hosted by Colorado State University, and supported by the Colorado State Univeristy Open Press, it brings together scholarly journals and book series as well as resources for teachers who use writing in their courses. This book is available in digital formats for free download at wac.colostate.edu.

Founded in 1965, the University Press of Colorado is a nonprofit cooperative publishing enterprise supported, in part, by Adams State University, Colorado State University, Fort Lewis College, Metropolitan State University of Denver, Regis University, University of Colorado, University of Northern Colorado, Utah State University, and Western State Colorado University. For more information, visit upcolorado.com.

CONTENTS

PREFACE

"One can probably never know all the sources influential in the process of writing a book . . ."

— George Hillocks, Jr., *Teaching Writing as Reflective Practice*

Very often when I read acknowledgments, I feel overcome. Especially when reading something like Donna Qualley's final note in her acknowledgments for *Turns of Thought*: "Finally, I want to acknowledge the important, complex, and at times disconcerting influence of my Grandmother Qualley. From her I learned how reading and writing are processes we can use to try to make sense of our worlds and ourselves. Twenty-five years after her death, I am still using reading and writing to make sense of her legacy to me" (xi). Qualley blends literacies with feeling, family, identity, loss and its aftereffects. I learn something about what drives her when I read this acknowledgment, something inaccessible in the rest of the book. Likewise, familiar texts that have become my thinking pals over the years, like Qualley's, surprised me as I got to know them differently, reading not for their main arguments but for their paratexts. When reading the stories about writing itself, I found that the worlds around texts frequently came into full bloom.

The most pleasurable part of writing this book was the time it granted me to read attentively the framing texts of others' books. In prefaces, introductions, dedications, and acknowledgments I have learned about writers' troubles, preoccupations, musical tastes, relationships, challenges, eating habits, animal companions, exercise routines, best friends, personal losses, and much more. Sometimes I found myself enjoying the frames more than the work they border (examples withheld), a feeling I suspect others share, as acknowledgments show us how writing gets made, or, not necessarily the same thing, how writers narrate the creation of writing. We also catch glimpses of how writers position themselves in relation to everything that surrounds and sprawls across writing. Here's Anne Ruggles Gere: "Cindy and Sam tolerated my long sessions with the computer but insisted that I keep up with their regular routines and join them for bike rides and skiing" (xiv). Lester Faigley's family gave him "the greatest support" and "space to finish the project" that became *Fragments of Rationality* despite misgivings about its content (xiii). John Schilb describes himself as "one of those writers, more numerous than you may think, who need music playing while they sit at the computer keyboard. Indeed, it is fair to say that many composers and performers have contributed to the making of this book, albeit indirectly" (ix). I can only hope that my rendering of writers' acknowledgments throughout this book does not squeeze the life out of these frequently extraordinary profiles of writers writing.

One effect of reading acknowledgments attentively, with intent to write about them, is a heightened consciousness of the genre, its surprises and riches, as well as its codified patterns of attribution. That consciousness, for me, has resulted in an avoidance of writing my own acknowledgments in this book for fear that my attempt will land with a resounding thud, a major disappointment given the attention I pay to this marginal genre in the following pages. In lieu of a separate acknowledgments section, which feels like too much pressure, my debts are threaded throughout the remainder of this preface.

Despite my own claims in this book about dispersed origins for any writing project, I couldn't resist trying to pinpoint when this project began. To do that, I looked back through my computer files and found one called "MMLAspecial-sessionproposal." This proposal for the 2012 MMLA, which was themed around the concept of "debt" and convened in my home city of Cincinnati, Ohio, is one starting point for this book. Several graduate students and I decided that we couldn't pass up the opportunity to attend this local conference. Our proposed session was approved; the abstract reads as follows:

> This session theorizes writing as an economy of indebtedness. We are interested in the following sorts of questions: How is writing mediated by the words of others? How do critical and creative writers implicitly and explicitly acknowledge the presence of others in their work? What's the relationship between influence and indebtedness? What role does affect play in acknowledging or refusing debts? Is indebtedness inherently backward-looking; is it possible to feel both indebted and to forge radical new directions? How can writing instruction benefit from an understanding of writing as entangled with indebtedness without miring novice writers in the long shadow of what's come before?

Rereading this, I notice how we defer making claims and instead pose a series of questions, confirming that, perhaps like many proposal writers, we were inventing a topic on the spot rather than creating a panel that coalesced around what we already knew. If it weren't for the conference and panel, titled "Writing and Indebtedness," I'm not sure that I would have written this book. While I wrote my portion of the panel from a place of some ambivalence—"Is this anything?" is for me a nagging question that plagues most of my scholarly writing—hearing the contributions from Allison Carr, Christina LaVecchia, Jason Nemec, and Hannah Rule planted a seed, made me realize we had stumbled into some very rich content worth mining more substantially. So, big gratitude to each of them for being inspiring, willing partners.

There were moments along the way when I thought I should abandon this project, got discouraged by skeptical feedback, or succumbed to nagging doubts about the value of yet another academic book out in the world. These concerns were in the back of my mind when I presented a portion of what became chapter four at the University of Wisconsin-Milwaukee Midwest Interdisciplinary Graduate Conference on "Animacy" in 2014. Facing an audience of skeptics, I stumbled. And then I began doubting the project. That experience, as it turns out, was a productive one for me, as the questions and comments helped me reenvision the framing of chapter four. Sometimes trouble helps, I guess, though I fully admit that sometimes it hurts in breathtaking ways. Anyway, thanks to the folks in Milwaukee, my graduate school stomping grounds, for taking the work seriously (despite its limitations), and especially to Alice Gillam, host and mentor extraordinaire.

This book demanded soundtracks. Writing's rhythms and percussive keyboarding can be, for me, stifling. Great music helped me get lost. I would have been excruciatingly lonely without the sonic awesomeness of The National, Waxahatchee, Sharon Van Etten, Andrew Bryant, Courtney Barnett, The Antlers, and so many others. Sometimes I imagined being in these and other bands . . . a fantasy release from writing. If I were a rock star, I wouldn't have to sit here hour after hour working out my thinking in slow motion . . . No, actually, I probably would.

I benefited from the company of others, including kitty companions Peanut (RIP; tears my heart out), Tiny (RIP), Oscar, Morrissey, and Pearly (RIP). Meows all around.

Students in the interdisciplinary dissertation workshop class that I taught during the summers of 2013–2016 were incredibly positive influences. We met for five hours a day for ten days to write together, taking breaks to talk, share, stretch, and eat. I wrote the book proposal and chapter one in the 2013 workshop, chapter two in 2014, chapter three in 2015, and am now revising the whole book in 2016.

I am grateful for permission from the National Council of Teachers of English (NCTE) to reprint excerpts from "Writing Material," originally published in *College English*, throughout this book. The article was part of a special issue on Reimagining the Social Turn, guest edited by Jacqueline Rhodes and Jonathan Alexander. J & J = dream team editors and aspirational colleagues. Thanks to them for seeing potential in that piece and including it alongside such great work.

Though I don't address the role of children in composing within these pages, I wrote this book with children near much of the time and wouldn't have it any other way. I'll always associate this book with Giovanni's guitar playing and Lou's soccer ball smacking the downstairs wall. Great music to write by. Also on the home front, I'm extremely grateful to Gary Weissman for his steady support, advice, amazing food, and near constant, welcome hilarity. When I thought I was done, he gently told me that I had to reorganize the first two chapters. This took the wind out of my sails, but I knew he was right and am thankful for his honesty. His expert reading and exacting feedback helped me clarify just about every sentence in here, or at least made me question what struck me as self evident, hopefully producing better thinking, better prose. Gary and I have been writing together for almost 20 years now; it seems to be working out!

Without the willing participants who completed my survey and contributed photos and narratives to the Facebook group, "Composing with Animals," chapter four would not have been possible in its present form. Big thanks for the time, care, and energy of all of my respondents, especially in this age of seemingly constant surveying. Likewise, participants at the 2014 Dartmouth Summer Seminar on Composition Research, especially Christiane Donahue, Neal Lerner, Chuck Bazerman, and Mya Poe, offered excellent advice and suggestions that directly shaped my research design and analysis. I'm so grateful for that humbling re-education in research methods and the supportive, smart community at Dartmouth.

External reviewers provided astonishingly generous and useful advice for creating a more coherent manuscript that progressively develops chapter-by-chapter. I don't know how I would have managed to make this book without their guidance. Editors Susan McLeod and Michael Palmquist offered productive commentary that helped me frame the book, unpack buried assumptions that informed my claims, and generally think more critically about audience expectations. Thanks for your belief and patience (all told, this project took three years). Thanks, too, to colleagues and students at Kansas State University and Ohio University, where I presented early versions of chapter three and gained insightful feedback that aided my subsequent drafting and revising. Special shout-out to Cydney Alexis and Mara Holt who organized those visits and offered smart feedback and excellent company.

A Taft Summer Research Fellowship in 2013 and a University Research Council Summer Research Fellowship in 2014, both through the University of Cincinnati, were hugely significant to my progress on this manuscript. Thanks to the dedicated faculty members who serve on those committees and who saw fit to support my work so generously.

Need I say that, even in the presence of many partners, all of this, finally, is my fault and my burden?

USAGE NOTE

I use "acknowledgments" rather than "acknowledgements" throughout this book, except when citing the latter usage in a direct quotation or a title. *Merriam-Webster's* allows for both variations; I chose the slightly shorter version for aesthetic reasons.

ACKNOWLEDGING
WRITING PARTNERS

INTRODUCTION
THAT GRATUITOUS SUPPLEMENT

"The study of acknowledgements is more hapless than most because the genre is only mandated to say a certain few things, and then in a socially proscribed way, according to conventionalized forms."

– Terry Caesar, "On Acknowledgements"

"I want to admit right away that no words I write are my own and that I never write alone."

– Tilly Warnock, "How I Write"

For some time now, I have turned to acknowledgments first in any book that I read. Writers' lives, work influences, and supports provide an intriguing back-story to a line of thought, a research project, and, in some cases, a lifelong obses-sion. Acknowledgments are the "Behind the Writing" of academic scholarship. Much like the VH1 program, "Behind the Music," acknowledgments can both numb with their sheer predictability and captivate by providing glimpses into a private world. At a minimum, acknowledgments give readers an inkling of how a writer came to develop a project, an approach, and, on rare occasions, the confidence to stand up for a particular idea or thesis.

The lure of peeking behind the curtain to see what warrants public gratitude and to learn about an author's influences is not exclusive to academics or writers, of course. In the liner notes to her 2012 album *Tramp*, singer-songwriter Sharon Van Etten thanks no less than 68 people and then names nearly 30 artists in a list of "recommended listening." A trail of breadcrumbs providing glimpses of the forces, affects, and cultural influences on her sound, the recommended list reads as a soundscape for the music she makes. More than a citational gesture, it permits mention of less immediately direct influences.

The desire to learn about strangers, their benefactors, predilections, wrong turns, and various experiences might be evidence of an insatiable cultural ap-petite for probing the intimacies of others' lives, for witnessing supposedly un-varnished "reality." Is it voyeuristic to go straight to acknowledgments before reading one word of the main text? Is the turn to the author's words about the writing process first driven by as banal a motivation as wanting access to the "real person" behind the writing? Such questions emerge from criticism of ac-knowledgments, but this study suggests that questions of this sort aren't particu-larly interesting because they fail to engage the complex writing realities offered through acknowledgments. They can be a straightforward list of funding sources or an inevitable expression of gratitude to a life-partner, but acknowledgments can also teach us how to feel about writing, depict beliefs and values associated with writing activity, and assert writing as cohabitation. The genre provides a unique view of writing practices and writers enmeshed in varying partnerships with others, organizations, niche groups, animals, and places.

My understanding of acknowledgments as a genre is dependent on their paratextual status. "Para," as J. Hillis Miller explains, "indicates alongside, near or beside" (441). Miller goes on to point out the ambiguity of "para" by detailing its competing significations; "para," he writes, is "at once proximity and distance, similarity and difference, interiority and exteriority, something at once inside a domestic economy and outside it, something simultaneously this side of the boundary line, threshold, or margin, and at the same time beyond it, equivalent in status and at the same time secondary or subsidiary, submissive, as of guest to host, slave to master" (441). Acknowledgments, following the articulation of "para" as neither inside nor outside, neither close nor distant, constitute a boundary, a "permeable membrane connecting inside and outside. . . an ambiguous transition between one and the other" (441). Gerard Genette, in *Paratexts: Thresholds of Interpretation*, similarly describes paratexts as threshold genres, but he adds authorial intent into the mix by articulating paratexts as forms that occupy a "fringe," which acts as "conveyor of a commentary that is authorial or more or less legitimated by the author" (2). Paratexts, Genette contends, are not obligatory for authors or readers: no one is required to write or read them, and their presence and presentation are influenced by prevailing conventions and context.

Their non-obligatory status might in fact be central to the appeal of acknowledgments, as reading them can feel recreational, intimate, and voyeuristic. At the same time, the non-obligatory status contrasts with the spatial prominence of acknowledgments: they consume prime real estate in a book—most often appearing before the main text—and yet, as described below in more detail, rarely are they treated as primary to a book's content or rhetorical power. In what follows, I discuss why writing scholars should care about acknowledgments, describe their evolution and key characteristics, outline how critics and essayists have treated the genre, and then describe this book's organization.

Before moving on, I want to note that, while my focus on writing partnerships as documented in acknowledgments is rooted in print texts—where acknowledgments most often appear—the wider genre set of paratexts is not exclusive to print. Paratextual elements of digital texts might include metadata, multi-user tag clouds, fan fiction, article-level metrics that document the number of times a piece has been viewed, cited, and/or downloaded, as well as hashtags and coding schemes that control web design and behavior. Such paratexts reveal dynamic writing partners in digital environments that fall outside the scope of my study but that indicate the larger genre set of which print acknowledgments are but a part. Because I focus on stories that writers tell about writing debts, my study is necessarily limited in scope.

ACKNOWLEDGMENT MATTER(S)

"Whenever I pick up a new (academic) book, I look at the acknowledgement page to see who shared in the experience of the authors in the creation of the work."

— Linda Adler-Kassner, *The Activist WPA*

"Why do we acknowledge only our textual sources but not the ground we walk, the ever-changing skies, mountains and rivers, rocks and trees, the houses we inhabit and the tools we use, not to mention the innumerable companions, both non-human animals and fellow humans, with which and with whom we share our lives? They are constantly inspiring us, challenging us, telling us things."

— Tim Ingold, *Being Alive*

I wrote my first acknowledgments in fifth grade. Mrs. Maher required us to include an acknowledgments page at the beginning of our research papers (she also required that we turn in note cards, which for me were handwritten on the inside of cereal boxes). My paper, long vanished from my parents' basement, was what would now be described as a heavily patch-written biographical study of Fredrick Douglass. I wish I could remember what I wrote in the acknowledgments, if I thanked the *Funk and Wagnall's Encyclopedia* set from which I borrowed so indiscriminately to complete that paper. Did I thank my parents or brother for helping me (surely they must have helped, though I have no recollection)? Did I thank the IBM typewriter set among piles of random papers on the basement table, right next to the seldom-used sewing machine? What remains in my memory is the strangeness I experienced when asked to thank others for a paper I thought was mine alone. That writing is never entirely "mine" or "alone"—an inescapable lesson emergent in written acknowledgments—constitutes a major premise of this book. Another is that the mini-narratives about writing delivered through acknowledgments provide provocative, though not necessarily truthful, views of writing as always *in the world*, not a secret activity at a remove from ordinary life, a persistent wrong impression that sticks to writing of any seriousness or import. In short, this book begins from the premise

5

that composition is communal and communing with, an activity never without partners, and that acknowledgments provide a particularly rich vantage point from which to make this claim.

If we seek an antidote to the misconception that writing is "mine alone," then reading acknowledgments does the trick. The act of acknowledging others, whether in the context of writing or life in general, is, in its ideal form at least, an ethical one. The gesture of acknowledging involves recognizing others and envisioning ourselves within relationships, as the following excerpt from an acknowledgment illustrates: "First, we thought we should thank the builders of web-based collaboration tools like Google Docs, Skype, and others. This collaboration—involving over 30 editors, contributors, and readers scattered across the United States and beyond—would not have been possible without them" (Harris, Miles, Paine ix). Here and elsewhere, the world in acknowledgments is the world of "we," composed of multiple partners who all contribute to something beyond the single-author self. "Partners," as I use the term, include humans, non-humans, matter, technology, animals, feelings, time, and a great many others.

This project takes a cue from new media scholars who have argued that studying ubiquitous technologies like the pencil, the page, and paper reveals the mundane and profound ways in which writing is always mediated by tools (e.g., Baron; Prendergast and Ličko; Trimbur and Press). In the midst of this turn to ordinary writing tools and scenes, focusing on acknowledgments right now has a logic to it. Acknowledgments are ubiquitous to academic writing even as they typically escape critical notice and are not treated as meaningful content in writing pedagogy (for an exception, see Harris, *Rewriting* 94–97). As a result, a vital, expressive economy of writing is mostly hidden in plain site. In acknowledgments, we see that writing activities are frequently mediated by diverse others, a mundane reality that allows for an expansive view of writing. Acknowledgments are a revealing lens through which to view writing as a practice of indebted partnerships in complex collaboration.

The epigraphs by Adler-Kassner and Ingold depict writing as an ecosystem that includes contributions from editors, friends, colleagues, animals, strangers, emotions, environments, and tools. In written acknowledgments, writers produce necessarily abbreviated narratives about the worlds of writing they create and/or inhabit and describe how they interact with each part of the ecosystem. These narratives and descriptions make explicit what might otherwise seem overly theoretical and removed from material circumstances: writing is curatorial in that writers are stewards of materials, which are arranged in deliberate ways to cohere with a guiding vision or purpose; distributed by way of multiple nodes of influence and production that together form a writing ecosystem; and immersed in fields of activity rather than bracketed as solitary activities produced separately from everyday life.

These qualities ascribed to writing have become familiar in composition studies, particularly as postprocess, multimodal, and new media understandings of writing and composing emerge and continue to be refined. Whereas new forms of writing and composing provide excellent opportunities for recognizing composing in the terms I've established above, the tendency to associate these qualities mostly with non-alphabetic texts elides the ways in which all composing can be understood as curatorial, distributed, and immersive. These are not categories unique to digital or multimodal composing, in other words. That said, the attention to new media and multimodal composing has generated productive reconsiderations of what counts as writing writ large, energizing the field's collective thinking about where and how to study writing.

Kendall Leon and Stacey Pigg's study of graduate student writing practices is a case in point. They argue that graduate student digital multitasking is writing that counts as real work, which they study using a mixed methods approach comprised of time-use diaries, screen captures, and interviews. For their research participants, writing is anything but single-minded: "Filling out forms is juxtaposed against creating academic knowledge through writing acts; checking email and connecting with friends, family, and acquaintances happens in the same moment as producing words that will eventually become presentations or publications" (8). Writing isn't a private activity, one that happens only in classrooms, heads, a room of one's own, or at kitchen tables, nor is it a set of linear tasks or a unimodal endeavor. It is elliptical, immersive in diverse environments, dispersed, ordinary (not rarified), mediated, ongoing, and coexistent with other activities. This idea shares kinship with Jody Shipka's research, which attaches value to writing's "broader flow of activity by highlighting the role other texts, people, activities, semiotic resources, institutions, memories, and motives play in the composers' overall production processes" (15).

For Shipka, the act of writing is not discrete but embedded in other forms of interaction and communing. A fitting example of this appears in Joseph Harris' acknowledgments for *A Teaching Subject*: "I wrote this book while teaching in the English department at the University of Pittsburgh; I doubt that I could have written quite the same book anywhere else, and I know I have learned more than I can say from the generous yet critically attentive talk about teaching that goes on there" (ix–x). The community of writers at the University of Pittsburgh constitutes what Shipka calls a "broader flow" that affects Harris' orientation to teaching. It often seems that documenting this "flow" is the express purpose of acknowledgments, an unusual site in academic writing where we see writing activities (the "doing") described and frequently narrativized, and writing recounted in retrospect, or in terms of writing's conditions of completion (the "done").

Acknowledgments provide rich source material for viewing composing as inhabited, located in time and place, and entangled in complex relationships with diverse others. In documenting this complexity, acknowledgments also depict something of the complicated act of writing, reminding me of Janet Emig's longing, stated in "The Uses of the Unconscious in Composing," for rhetoric and writing guides of the 1960s to at least gesture toward "the untidy . . . the convoluted . . . the not-wholly-known . . . a more intricate self and process" (48). Some of these qualities of composing do in fact emerge in acknowledgments, a site that invites writing about writing and frequently documents the dispersed activities that constitute writing.

At the same time, I realize that acknowledgments invite mockery, affirming their literal and symbolic marginal status based on overdetermined generic tendencies. That is, the excessive performative qualities of acknowledgments make it hard to read them as trustworthy sites through which to understand writing. This point hit home for me when I applied for a grant to support this project. In their rejection letter, committee members wrote, "The project appears to take acknowledgments at face value, as an indicator of the writer's process or environment but these are often used strategically or even disingenuously—to pay social niceties, to thank loved ones who were not in fact helpful, to construct falsely humble narratives." This criticism, echoed in critiques of acknowledgments more broadly, and recounted below, helped me realize that I am not concerned with veracity in acknowledgments. I am interested in the stories that writers construct about writing—true or otherwise—because the choices result in crafted narratives that reveal what writing is like or perhaps what it should be like under ideal circumstances. In other words, fabrications and puffery, as well as the truth about writing, bring to light both real and imagined writing partnerships; rather than try to distinguish between fiction and reality, I read acknowledgments as archives flush with stories about writing.

Acknowledgments are micro-economies of debt and praise. This book explores those economies and proposes a lexical and conceptual shift from "writing about" to "writing with." Following from contemporary critical theory in fields as diverse as animal studies, new media studies, biology, anthropology, and political theory, there is a discernible shift toward conceiving and studying various phenomena as inseparable from objects, technologies, animals, sensory elements, and other partners. This work has helped me view writing as codependent with a host of others and to resist separatist thinking in order to imagine how to talk and think about writing as an indiscreet art. My study of writing is not dependent on current theories exclusively, though. The seeds for this project were planted some time ago by composition scholars, a lineage detailed in the next chapter and followed by a discussion of what writing partners, as made visible in acknowledgments, connote in this study. First, though, I outline academic and popular treatments of acknowledgments with a particular focus on constructs of writing that emerge from this genre.

CONTEXTUALIZING ACKNOWLEDGMENT STUDIES

Scholars generally agree that writing was created as a form of accounting, or record-keeping, around the 4th millennium BC in response to a changing economy (cf. Robinson). Acknowledgments might be seen as a direct descendent of this originating use of writing. Essentially writing about writing, acknowledgments are a form of accounting in an ever-changing economy of writing, one that catalogs debts and credits, typically (and hopefully) with more prosaic appeal than might a straightforward ledger. Whether they name granting institutions, venues where previous work was published, mentors, friends, family, students, or seemingly far-flung recipients like the natural world or pets, and whether sincere or full of bunk, acknowledgments document services, exchanges, flows of capital (human, monetary, and otherwise), as well as a writer's view of writing practices. As such, they function as a lens for understanding how writing is practiced, experienced and, implicitly, defined. They also tell us something about the economy in which writing circulates, and, by that standard, demonstrate that writing is always "writing with" something beyond the self.

Most critical analyses of and commentaries on acknowledgments were published in the 1990s, though, as I discuss in the next section, research by international scholars has begun to appear with more regularity in the past five years. The timing of the initial research on acknowledgments converges with the rise of social constructionism across the disciplines and its insistence on the social make-up of language, identity, reality, meaning, and a whole range of practices and phenomena. This movement laid the groundwork for Blaise Cronin's claim, in his 1995 book on acknowledgments, whimsically titled *The Scholar's Courtesy*, that "research and writing are socially embedded processes" (1). Intellectual work, from this point of view, is never divorced from social scenes and associated people, things, and structures in those scenes. His study, like others produced during the same time period, emphasizes the pervasiveness of social exchange to scholarship. Collaboration, conversations with peers, presentations at conferences, and discussion with students, for example, all contribute to and enrich one's thinking.

Of course, peer influences might be construed more cynically in the context of acknowledgments. For example, Cronin and his coauthor Kara Overfelt surveyed readers of academic texts in 1992 and found that, while over 50%

read acknowledgments, frequently as a way to gauge relevance of an essay or book to their own research, 87.1% read them to register whether or not they themselves were acknowledged (171). This contrast in reader practices illuminates academics' usually unspoken desire to receive praise and recognition and paints acknowledgments as little more than reciprocal backscratching, an overdetermined genre composed of limited content that adheres to a static formula.

The perceived conformity of acknowledgments was no doubt made more apparent by social constructionism, which, among other things, buoyed the basis for understanding genres as "an index to cultural patterns" and "keys to understanding how to participate in the action of a community," as Carolyn Miller contends in her 1984 study of genre as rhetorical action (165). Social construction, a critical standpoint that achieved near automaticity throughout the 1980s and 1990s, made it routine to proclaim that everything is a social construction and that inherent characteristics are only made to seem so through complex discursive processes, often inflected by political and ideological stances. Meanwhile, poststructuralism, an influential critical orientation during the same period, emphasized the power of discourse to shape reality and rejected grand narratives, valuing instead plural, small-scope narratives as a better gauge for analyzing the intersectional complexity of, for instance, class inequality, women's disempowerment, and race-based inequities.

In addition, deconstruction—poststructuralism's methodology and theory of reading—taught a whole generation of scholars to be wary of dichotomies (male/female; center/margin; heterosexual/homosexual) and the hierarchical valuation they (re)produce. As Derrida argued so effectively, dichotomies privilege one term and subordinate its other. Deconstructionists showed how focusing on a seemingly minor aspect of a text could disrupt binary logic, unraveling the hierarchical relationship established by that dualistic slash. Deconstructive readings often involved undoing the binarism of center/margin by drawing attention to previously marginal textual elements.

It doesn't seem a coincidence that, in this critical environment, acknowledgments became an object of study, even if only a minor one. They are, after all, peripheral to the main text, and typically considered less important to its meaning and function. As Terry Caesar puts it, acknowledgments are "presumably 'outside' the book, the 'text proper'" (92). They are even more outside the text proper than citations, which have been the subject of considerably more research since the 1960s and into the present. Citations can be counted and analyzed to gauge influences, trends in coauthorship, and biases in a field of study. Some search engines, like EBSCOhost and Google Scholar, include citation-tracking information, making it possible to trace how an article or author has influenced a given field by indicating the number of times both have been cited and in what sources. Readers can also learn which scholars' articles have been cited with the most frequency. Web of Knowledge offers similar information in addition to citation mapping, an article's list of works cited, and, where available, direct links to cited articles.

By contrast, acknowledgments and their personal content present time-consuming difficulties for large-scale research projects. Acknowledgments do not conform to bibliometrics, statistical analyses of authorship, publication, and citation patterns. Representing a much less systematic and unquantifiable measure of influence and impact, particularly within humanities research, acknowledgments are not easily traceable. (A notable exception, AckSeer, an acknowledgment indexer for scientific literature, is a search engine that extracts content from acknowledgments for indexing and analysis.)

Whereas citation analyses put a face on research trends, acknowledgments put a face on writing, authors, and their surround. Poststructuralism decentered the author, famously posited the author as dead (Barthes), which may account for the less than enthusiastic development of acknowledgment studies, in which authors are ever-present. Indeed, poststructuralism emphasized fragmented, discursively constructed explanations of problems, mirroring its position on the fragmentation of a coherent self. The decentered subject was described in terms of subject positions, understood as constructed in and through language. Acknowledgments, by contrast, position the author as an important and real component of knowledge making, moving her out of the shadowy subject position and into the role of writer/person engaged with materials, others, and environments. The study of acknowledgments, and their steadily increasing presence in scholarly books, suggests that the author has found in textual gutters a sanctioned space where she can depict writing as an immersive, distributed, companionate activity.

CRITICAL VIEWS

> "If your book has its origins in a dissertation, your acknowledgments
> should not draw attention to this fact, as it will discourage library sales
> and book review attention."
>
> — *The University of Chicago Press*

Acknowledgments became common only in the 1960s, as noted by Ken Hyland. Writing in 2003, Hyland contextualizes the genre's emergence as follows:

> Academic tomes have always contained expressions of grati-
> tude, and in journal publishing, early scientific articles often

> featured acknowledgements in an introductory cover letter
> (Atkinson, 1999). Their emergence as a textual feature was
> uneven until the 1940s . . . , and while they are still to be
> found in book prefaces or article footnotes, the compulsion to
> recognize colleagues and funding bodies is now more likely to
> receive institutional endorsement and editorial prominence in
> a separate textual space. ("Dissertation" 244)

In addition to appearing in prefaces and footnotes, acknowledgments might take form as an author's note or a dedication at the beginning of a text. I use this loose framing of the genre's emergence as a point of orientation since identifying an exact origin point for acknowledgments and the forms they have taken is beyond the scope of this project. Such mapping, in fact, exceeds the reach of existing research. That is, to my knowledge there is no comprehensive transdisciplinary study of acknowledgments in critical books (though discipline-specific ones exist, as discussed below); no complete tracking of their history and evolution; no longitudinal studies that might reveal, for instance, the traces of gender politics or other reflections of social arrangements in these sometime-juicy paratexts. Thus, my analysis proceeds by focusing on acknowledgments where they emerge: mostly as a freestanding genre appearing at the beginning of a book, which Hyland dates to sometime in the 1960s, less often at the end of prefaces or in other front matter.

Acknowledgments have been described variously as a record of "hidden influencers" (Cronin, Scholar's 1), a space where academics reveal themselves as "total persons not limited to their professional selves" (Ben-Ari 78), a pastoral genre that mixes high and low registers (Caesar 88), "a curious achievement of pretension, hyperbole and banality" (Hamilton 2), and a "Cinderella," "optional," and "interactional" genre (Hyland, "Dissertation"). As these descriptors suggest, when acknowledgments are discussed—which is not often—they personify extremes of a curious sort. Whether maligned for indecorous self-promotion or grating deference to superiors, or valued for the authentic space they provide academics seeking to prove they are in fact "regular" people, acknowledgments are deliciously ambivalent scholarly material.

I assumed this fertile genre would have generated a range of analyses—particularly from feminist and rhetorical genre studies perspectives, given that acknowledgments blur distinctions between private and public (feminist interest), and represent a paratextual genre in action (rhetorical genre studies). After some initial research, however, I was surprised to find that, while existing work is rigorous and significant, there's not much of it. Studies of academic acknowledgments as textual forms have been largely limited to the fields of information science, anthropology, and linguistics, though acknowledgments in popular texts have been the subject of periodic pieces in venues like *The Economist* and *The New York Times*. While the former have offered rigorous studies of the genre and its field-specific conventions, including its role in academic identity formation and community membership, the latter have tended to indict acknowledgments as narcissistic, fictionalized descriptions of writers' lives, complete with supportive, understanding spouses, patient children, helpful editors, clean-working publishing houses, generous university support, and other unlikelihoods coaxed by the euphoria of completion or the immodesty of careerism.

Among the earliest studies of acknowledgments I have found are a 1972 unpublished dissertation on patterns of acknowledgment in sociology (Macintosh) and a 1991 study of acknowledgment practices in genetics (McCain). Really, though, Blaise Cronin, professor of information science at Indiana University, is largely responsible for making acknowledgments an explicit object of study. Since 1991, Cronin, often with coauthors, began to conduct empirical studies of acknowledgments, approaching them as a lens for examining the role of mentors in the development of scholarship ("Let"), patterns of personal attribution within library science journals (Cronin, McKenzie, Stiffler), field-specific genre norms (Cronin, McKenzie, Rubio), the social embeddedness of writing (*Scholar's*), and, more recently, collaborative work practices in the arts and sciences ("Collaboration"). In his 1995 *The Scholar's Courtesy*, Cronin distinguishes between acknowledgments and citations by writing that the latter develop an intellectual lineage of sorts, while acknowledgments foreground a "private interaction, or debt" (25). He notes that both "declare a relationship between the author and other actors on the academic stage," but acknowledgments are "a voluntary act of reciprocation" (25). The book argues for valuing acknowledgments as evidence of the social exchange necessary to create scholarship. Going further, Cronin seeks to concretize this value by including it in what he calls the "Reward Triangle (authorship, citation, acknowledgement)" (27). Acknowledgments, he argues, should count in promotion and tenure cases as evidence of influence and impact, a position that strikes me as untenable in relation to this idiosyncratic, optional genre, and undesirable too, since formalizing the value of acknowledgments might increase the genre's tendency toward rote expression and professional obligation and, frankly, force it to become less of a wild card.

Lest I give the impression that Cronin is fixated on rewards, I want to make clear that he attributes a wide range of functions to acknowledgments, writing that they can be viewed as "indicators of hidden influences" or as "gifts," "tokens of esteem," "credits or rewards," and, intriguingly, "ritualistic appendages" (about which the next section will have more to say) (18). The bigger picture, Cronin writes, is that acknowledgments help to "locate the author(s) in a particular cognitive or social milieu" and to assert group identity (19). To substantiate his claims, he conducts an empirical study of ten years of acknowledgments in ten high impact sociology journals, a classification established by Reuters' Journal Citation Reports. Comparing citation and acknowledgment data, Cronin finds that the two, at least in sociology, do not necessarily correlate: "one is visible and its influence measurable through citations; the other, historically hidden, is potentially detectable through the study of acknowledgements" (79). Not terribly surprising results, but when Cronin drilled down further to study transdisciplinary attitudes about acknowledgments, he made some interesting discoveries.

His study, mailed to 1,000 academics in 1993, yielded 278 valid responses from faculty in various disciplines across ranks (majority at associate or full), with 81.7% from men and 15.5% from women (remainder unknown). Though he largely downplays and even seems reluctant to address the significance of gender differences, Cronin found that women more often than men felt that they deserved an acknowledgment but didn't receive one. Acknowledgments, in the women's accounts, are intertwined with questions of suspected plagiarism of their work by male colleagues. One woman reports that she did receive an acknowledgment even though coauthor status was actually more appropriate: "'Yes, I once received an acknowledgement when a colleague submitted a paper that was about a 1/3 paraphrase of my own unpublished paper. It may be relevant that I had been sleeping with him'" (87). Another notes the following:

> 'This happened frequently to me and I believe to other
> women as well. I could cite many instances among them: (1)
> co-authors who in joining projects expect to receive a co-au-
> thor status in *my* write-ups but who think they would single
> author their write-ups (even where I am the senior partner in
> the project); (2) people who think that co-authoring with me
> licenses them to lift my work and re-use it forever more with
> nothing more than an acknowledgement, etc.' (87)

These by-now familiar-sounding charges echo reports of sexism (and racism, ableism, ageism) that have been widely reported in the years since Cronin's 1995 book (i.e., Ahmed, *On Being*; Berry and Mizelle; Gutiérrez y Muhs et al.). Cronin's research, however, helps to shed light on how the study of acknowledgments speaks to the politics of scholarship. As he puts it, acknowledgments are "not trivial, meta-textual flourishes" (98), but "constitute a potentially rich source of insight into the rules of engagement which define the bases of collaboration, social exchange and interdependence within academia" (108). In the above examples, the rules of engagement are organized by gendered and sexualized power differentials that get reenacted in acknowledgments.

In another article, Cronin and his coauthors develop a composite of acknowledgments drawn from scholarly journals in the disciplines of history, philosophy, psychology, and sociology over a twenty-year period. They identify six prominent topics appearing with regularity in the genre: moral support, financial support, access, clerical support, technical support, and peer interactions (Cronin, McKenzie, Rubio 31). Their research convincingly reveals networks of tangible and intangible support that undergird academic scholarship, making clear that writers are not, and never have been, lone wolves, however appealingly romantic that image might be. In his recent scholarship, Cronin argues that the lone wolf is becoming "something of an endangered species, having been displaced by groups, ensembles, and distributed collaborations" ("Collaboration" 22).

Distributed authorship has been fairly normative in the sciences for some time now, as Cronin points out, though not always without conflict. In 1991, the *New England Journal of Medicine* developed guidelines to rein in the increasing length and wide berth of acknowledgments, particularly in the context of multicenter clinical trials (Kassirer and Angell 1511). The editors cite an example of a twelve-page manuscript they accepted in which five pages were dedicated to acknowledgments (1511). The acknowledgments "listed 63 institutions and 155 physicians, the number of patients each institution had contributed (some as few as one), the 51 members of seven different committees, their institutions and their specialties, and the secretaries in the trial office. Many persons were named on more than one committee" (1511). As a result of such page-hungry acknowledgments, the editors developed guidelines limiting the genre to 600 words; those in excess were to be placed on record with the National Auxiliary Publications Service (1512).

In the humanities and social sciences, acknowledgments occupy a different place of importance. Writing in 1987, Eyal Ben-Ari, for example, views anthropologists' use of acknowledgments through the context of their scholarly training. Attributing the often-personal acknowledgments that anthropologists publish to a desire to "create images of ethnographers as social persons" (76), Ben-Ari notes that their intellectual interests in home cultures create a "persistent 'need' to express something about their relations with others" (78). Describing the world of ethnographers in the 1960s as characterized by asymmetrical power relations between students and advisors (71), Ben-Ari reveals the underlife of acknowledgments, where power differentials are woven into expressions of gratitude, as the following example illustrates: "And then I must thank Professor Evans-Pritchard, a more austere teacher, who teaches all his students that the study of man should be approached not necessarily without emotion but with careful scientific impartiality" (qtd. in Ben-Ari 70).

15

Linguist Ken Hyland, in his 2000 *Disciplinary Discourses*, focuses on how academics collaborate through texts. He notes, "Writers are oriented to more than an immediate encounter with their text when composing; they also conjure up institutional patterns which naturally and ideologically reflect and maintain such patterns" (xi). What's visible here are the limitations of an exclusively cognitive or muse-inspired approach to writing. For Hyland, writers always write in partnership with larger academic conventions and expectations. While the following chapters expand the concept of partnership to include much more than norms of discourse communities, Hyland's study provides a useful foundation for that discussion. Likewise, in "Dissertation Acknowledgements: The Anatomy of a Cinderella Genre" (2003), Hyland offers a genre specific analysis of dissertation acknowledgments that establishes a rhetorical approach to the genre helpful to my thinking throughout this work. He studies "professional connections and relationships as well as the valued disciplinary ideals of modesty, gratitude, and appropriate self-effacement" (266). Acknowledgments, he contends, are an "optional" and "interactional" genre, one that reveals "patterns of engagement that define collaboration and interdependence among scholars, and the practices of expectation and etiquette that are involved" (244).

More recent scholarship on acknowledgments by international scholars explores collaboration, etiquette, and other factors in relation to diverse material conditions, most often through a linguistic lens. In *Chinese PhD Thesis Acknowledgements*, for instance, Hua Peng uses survey and interview data to better understand acknowledgment practices of interdisciplinary Chinese writers, such as the frequency with which "Classic Chinese" students thanked those who shared reference materials with them. Peng concludes that these acknowledgments reflect culture-specific research conditions. Because these writers are working with materials that are centuries old or published outside China, the ability to lay hands on them is extremely compromised. Thus, when others assist with access, researchers make significant mention in acknowledgments. To depict typical problems of access, Peng writes,

> I read an acknowledgment text saying that her request of reference book was declined because at the time it was very humid and the reference book could not be exposed to such humid air. . . .A similar example referred to a reference book which was not allowed to be photocopied for fear of any possible damage to the rare edition. The student had to copy the book by hand in the library for days. (183)

In another effort to draw distinctions between Peng's research participants and Hyland's Westerners, Peng notes that "name dropping" may be expected by Western researchers, but such naming in Chinese culture could be "a face-threatening act for the acknowledged who does not want to be mentioned as such on such a public occasion" (215).

In a comparative study of "soft sciences" dissertation acknowledgments written by native speakers of Persian (NSP) and native speakers of English (NSE), Mohammad Javad Mohammadi, also building on Hyland's research, analyzes rhetorical moves and "steps" that structure acknowledgments (536). While he finds considerable similarities between the two groups, he identifies one significant difference: the NSP writers employ what he calls the "thanking God" step to a much higher degree than do the NSE writers (80% of Persian texts compared to 4% of English ones) (543). Mohammadi explains this move in terms of cultural difference: "Since in the Islamic culture everyone is usually assumed to start work by the name of God and finish it by thanking God, so it is quite natural if such a step is to be found even in dissertation acknowledgements" (543).

Also comparing Western and non-Western approaches to acknowledgments, María Ángeles Alcaraz examines research articles in neurology to contrast acknowledgments written by English and Spanish writers. Her study is focused on collaboration practices as made visible in acknowledgments. While English writers devote more space to thanking granting institutions, Spanish writers spend significantly less, suggesting that "less funds [are] devoted to research, development and innovation, by national and local institutions" where Spanish-speaking researchers conduct their research (125).

In total, this work provides important reminders that acknowledgments—all texts, really—are cultural records that relay something about a particular group of people and the political, intellectual, economic, and cultural environment they inhabit (for more international studies of acknowledgments, see Giannoni; Golpour; Mingwei and Yajun). It also provides a fascinating portrait of writers writing, adding more dimension and significance to acknowledgments, a paratext through which we glean contextual clues about realities that control and influence the larger work. In this sense, depictions of acknowledgments as boorish, self-aggrandizing publicity—a frequent charge, as illustrated in the next section—fail to account for the way acknowledgments can render the material, emotional, and social elements of knowledge making in cultural contexts.

POPULAR VIEWS OF ACKNOWLEDGMENTS

When we pay attention to acknowledgments, Terry Caesar notes, we come away with a sense that the work, "like its author, takes its place in larger human rhythms which embrace both past and future" (93). Acknowledgments humanize knowledge making, casting it in "the warm glow of an intimate con-

17

versation" (Caesar 88). They also provide glimpses of how books are made at a particular moment in time, as when, for instance, writers thank "squads of research teams, librarians, graduate students, government agencies, and private foundations" (Epstein 43), as well as illustrators, publishers, computer programs and programmers, social media, copy editors, marketing teams, and so forth. In this way, acknowledgments are potential barometers of writing and publishing technologies.

They are also, as noted above, spaces where the author is unabashedly front and center. The author's irrepressible presence, in fact, is precisely the problem for some critics of the genre writ-large (i.e, not particular to academic acknowledgments). In a *New York Times* article, "The Mistakes in This Essay Are My Own," John Maxwell Hamilton surveys 50 random books on his shelves and finds them to be filled with formulaic banalities that he compares to "kids cobbl[ing] together Mr. Potato Head" (2). Questioning the credibility of authors as they present themselves in acknowledgments, Hamilton asks, "How, indeed, does one measure authors who see around them only unfailingly helpful librarians, cheerful typists, utterly candid sources and selfless scholars who, contrary to the reality of academe, always make constructive comments—and on time?" (2).

In a similar vein, "Gratitude that Grates," an anonymous op-ed in *The Economist*—published in the 1990s as was Hamilton's piece—contends that in acknowledgments writers produce "long, rambling essays, in which they flatter the powerful, gurgle over their families, and otherwise boast to the world what happily married, highly-educated, well-connected and generally right-on people they have the good fortune to be" (83). Joseph Epstein too suggests that praise and gratitude are rendered nearly compulsive within the genre of acknowledgments. As he puts it, "Once [writing acknowledgments has] begun, it is not easily brought to a close, for it is something akin to handing out gratuities with play money—one may as well be a big spender" (43).

More recently, we seem to be awash in anti-acknowledgment sentiment. For instance, Noreen Malone, writing in the *New Republic*, uses the publication of Sheryl Sandberg's call for women to assume leadership roles in American corporations issued in *Lean In* as an occasion for railing against what she calls a "truly endemic and toxic" cultural phenomenon. She refers not to the prevalence of bullying, pedophilia, racist violence, legislative stalemates, or gun violence in American culture, but to the "current state of the 'Acknowledgments' section, what has perhaps reached its nadir in Sandberg's work. Lean in, and drop a name." Noting that Sandberg's acknowledgments consume seven-and-a-half pages and thank "140 people for contributing to her 172 page book," Malone laments the "exegeses of just how each person helped." And she's not alone in her distress about the excessiveness of Sandberg's acknowledgments. In *The Awl*,

Choire Sicha, extrapolating from Sandberg's book to make a point about the wider publishing industry, charges that book acknowledgments "have gone absolutely bonkers."

Malone points to other recent texts with similarly long acknowledgments—all of which, not coincidentally, are written by famous or semi-famous, well-connected people—and curses the name-dropping, sucking-up habits of contemporary acknowledgments. She approvingly excerpts an email response on the topic from *Paris Review* editor Lorin Stein, who complains, "'You don't see Joseph Conrad thanking Ford Madox Ford, or Virginia Woolf giving shout-outs to Leonard, Lytton, Vanessa, Clive, and Vita.'" Excessive acknowledging, he continues, "'mars the real intimacy of a novel, which is—or should be—between writer and reader and nobody else.'" This idea is echoed in a 2012 *New Yorker* piece by Sam Sacks, in which he charges that "[w]riters who saw themselves as magi, practitioners of mysterious art, would never have dreamed of breaking the spell they'd cast by guilelessly stepping out of character to thank their house pets."

Stein and Sacks' comments cut to the heart of the matter. Writing is supposed to be a private affair—creative writing in particular—that depends on a cloistered, never quite revealed, let alone discussed, contract between writer and reader. From this view, books are spells whose magic works only if we never catch a glimpse of what or who lies behind the curtain. The writer perverts good taste by airing too much insider information about the act of writing a book, a point that Sacks underscores: "Perhaps readers already know that book publishing is an insular, back-scratching industry, but does it have to be revealed quite so openly?" In an online comment, a reader concurs, comparing acknowledgments in novels (second in offense only to those in "scholarly books") to "a bloody accident in the street (or perhaps a burst sewer main)." While these examples are neither equivalent nor to scale, the point is clear: authors should refrain from making spectacles of themselves. More modesty equals more magic.

What really seems to incense Sacks, though, is the promotional character of acknowledgments, a genre that "appears like an online pop-up ad" or "an extension of the book's publicity" and is plagued by a politician-like appeal to "crowd-pandering." For Sacks, acknowledgments are an unsolicited "gratuitous supplement" that is "garrulously narcissistic and strewn with clichés." I have to admit that his hostility to the genre puzzled me at first. There are terrible things happening in the world everyday; why direct so much ire to a "gratuitous supplement"? Then it dawned on me that the anger is about the disappearance of the magi from the literary scene. Here we should recall that his target is not academic acknowledgments but the rise of the over-exposed, non-enigmatic Novelist. Sacks explains that the "heyday of the literary auteur is long past, replaced by the era of the writing program." The result, for him, is a loss of "mystique in a craft" and the "quiet needed to disappear into a novel." Despite all that's been said to debunk the writer-in-the-garret myth, Sacks dares you to take it once and for all from his cold dead hands.

Writing against this rarified notion of book-making, *Slate* contributor David Haglund offers a more pragmatic stance on the issue. Writers can scroll acknowledgments to find an agent, for example, or to learn about book-making processes. "The real inspiration for a work of literary art may be mysterious," Haglund contends, "but the process by which that work reaches us should not be. Transparency is good. And so is gratitude."

Gratitude gone too far is the subject of historian Claire Potter's 2006 commentary on acknowledgments published in *The Chronicle of Higher Education*. Writing about academic acknowledgments, Potter calls to mind orgasmic release as she wonders if writers feel "embarrassed from some of the declarations of love made so thoughtlessly at a time when the relief at being finished with the book was so overwhelming everyone and everything seemed dear to them." She shifts metaphors, asserting that acknowledgments have "metastasized," evoking the spread of life-threatening cancer cells as an apt characterization of changing acknowledgment practices. Potter came to this view after completing her research for a book that entailed examining historical texts published before 1930. Tracing the shifts in acknowledgment practices in a casual way, she reports that the 1980s brought a noticeable uptick in the length and a loosening of beliefs about relevant content to be included in the genre (as reported above, Hyland locates the uptick in the 1960s; these may be field-specific differences). Potter identifies reality TV as one possible culprit affecting the inflation of academic acknowledgments, asserting "there is no realm of relationship that we automatically feel comfortable keeping private any more." In addition, though, Potter connects the increase of acknowledgments to the state of the profession, particularly to the growing need for scholars to network, attend conferences, and essentially build alliances with faculty at other institutions in preparation for heightened tenure and promotion requirements.

To reduce the problem as she sees it, Potter offers a list of categories that writers should "eliminate or trim" from acknowledgments. The top offender is mention of pets ("they just do pet things"), followed by gratitude for "ordinary human relationships" that do not contribute to "scholarly thought" (in this category, she includes "manicurists, personal trainers, the rowing club," and so forth). From there, she nixes mention of family members "doing what family is supposed to do under ordinary circumstances"; friends; scholars whose work has been influential ("utterly shameless"); insider references; and children. Apparently, "scholarly thought," separate from ordinary life, is indebted only to editors and publishing houses, a matter that I'll take up later in this book.

Potter's essay generated two online comments. One is from Anthony Grafton, author of *The Footnote* who, as you might guess, is predisposed to care about marginal genres. The other is from "Flavia," who confesses that the "excessive and self-promoting" tendencies of acknowledgments are in fact appealing. She worked for an academic publisher and admits that even when she was unlikely to know anyone mentioned, she "turned to the acknowledgements first and read them straight through. It's like reading the wedding announcements, or those horrible Christmas newsletters that many people send out—often awful, but still, somehow, compelling." Acknowledgments, Flavia points out, reveal "how people construct those lives within a public and relatively formal genre like the acknowledgements section." In reply, Potter confesses that she too always reads them first "to put off thinking for as long as possible"; also, she directs her students to read acknowledgments "to get a sense of the web of intellectual connections between books and readers."

The dominant take-away from Potter's essay, and the others described above, is that acknowledgments consolidate writers' least likable traits. Acknowledgments become emblematic of the narcissistic tendencies of contemporary culture while unveiling the mundane practicalities of writing. The latter might be the worst offense, according to current critics of acknowledgments, for the long-windedness of the genre gives too much away. It both destroys the mystique of writing and unleashes too much feeling, especially hyperbolic confessions of love and gratitude.

OF SUPPLEMENTS

While reading these accounts, I began thinking about the "gratuitous supplement" moniker as more potentially significant than the implied dismissal first appeared. It returned me to Derrida's discussion of "that dangerous supplement," which references Jean-Jacques Rousseau's description of writing in contrast to speech. Rousseau viewed writing as a dangerous supplement to speech, a perversion of the natural act of speech by the cultural inscription of writing. Yet, as Derrida points out, we only know Rousseau through his writing. For Derrida, to view writing as supplement to speech is to valorize presence and to reinforce false oppositions between speech and writing (adhering to what Derrida terms logocentricism). Texts are ultimately chains of supplements with no single point of origin at their center, no presence to ground an authentic experience of reading and interpretation. The supplement, writes Derrida, is "*exterior*, outside of the positivity to which it is super-added, alien to that which, in order to be replaced by it, must be other than it" (145). The supplement's perversion of nature—its constant deferral of origins—is seductive because, as Derrida explains, the supplement leads "desire away from the good path, makes it err far from natural ways, guides it toward its loss or fall and therefore it is a sort of lapse or scandal" (151). The seduction further emphasizes alienation from nature through an "infinite chain, ineluctably multiplying the supplementary mediations that produce the sense of the very thing they defer: the mirage of the thing itself, of immediate presence, of originary perception. Immediacy is derived" (157). Supplementarity is for Derrida the state of things; there is no original Presence, nothing Natural that a supplement supplements.

In light of Derrida's provocative claims, it's plausible to consider that behind the critiques outlined above is a sense that acknowledgments pose a danger by seducing our attention and interest away from what should be the primary content of a text and toward exteriority—the world beyond the text often made visible in the pages of acknowledgments. The demanding presence of acknowledgments might be evidence that the main text is not, after all, *main*. Not autonomous or entirely original, not magical but cultural, social, historical—the main text does not stand on its own. A book is undermined or in some way destabilized by its supplement, which is, in this case, acknowledgments. They threaten to seduce the reader away from the real content, and toward the conditions of its formation. As a permeable boundary between the interior and exterior of a text, acknowledgments occupy a liminal state, potentially distracting the reader with glimpses of the real and mundane, thereby threatening the idea that "the work" stands on its own.

METHODS OF READING ACKNOWLEDGMENTS

"Even if you sit in a tiny room in a tiny town hundreds of kilometers from the center of the world and don't meet a single soul, their hell is your hell, their heaven is your heaven, you have to burst the balloon that is the world and let everything in it spill over sides."

– Karl Ove Knausgaard, *My Struggle*

"We didn't have husbands who typed the manuscript nor children who played quietly while we worked, but we still have a few people whose help and support we'd like to acknowledge. . . . "

– Pat Belanoff and Marcia Dickson, *Portfolios: Process and Product*

Susan Sontag's tribute to writer Paul Goodman, published in 1972, begins, "I am writing this in a tiny room in Paris, sitting on a wicker chair at a typing table in front of a window which looks onto a garden; at my back is a cot and a night table; on the floor and under the table are manuscripts, notebooks, and two or three paperback books" (3). Sontag is not alone. She is surrounded by physical and environmental things and framed by the structure of place—a room, Paris, a garden. Every morning, she receives the *Herald Tribune* and its American news, calling to her mind very specific responses: "the B-52s raining ecodeath on Vietnam, the repulsive martyrdom of Thomas Eagleton, the paranoia of Bobby Fischer, the irresistible ascension of Woody Allen, excerpts from the diary of Arthur Bremer—and, last week, the death of Paul Goodman" (4). These others populate her serene writing getaway, even if not physically in the room with her. In this sense, composing is never something we do alone; we may do it in privacy, but sentences always tumble from a populated mind, heart, body, world.

A critical reading of acknowledgments helps us to understand and appreciate writing as populated and, along the way, to uncover ineffable truths about writing not immediately accessible on the surface or in the content of an argument, proposition, or claim. Writing activity is indexed in acknowledgments, which connote material in the many ways that term can signify: documentation of physical and non-physical matter from which research is made; sometime testament to what is essential in the making of a work; and reflection of the constituents—or raw materials—of a made thing. The genre storehouses compulsory and non-compulsory forms of gratitude and debt. Barbara Couture's explanation of writerly debts correlates to compulsory expressions in acknowledgments: "[W]riters must attend to the world outside themselves in order to effectively link one human being to another. This is what is required to be accountable as a writer" (35). Compulsory forms include thanking a dissertation director, reviewer, and/or copy editor, while non-compulsory ones can include thanking animals, exercise, food, travel, and so forth. Non-compulsory debts could be perceived as deviant because they appear distant from writing when conceived as a literal practice of producing words, yet they appear with some regularity in acknowledgments, despite the fact that they tap into no existing academic reward system.

Reading the compulsory and non-compulsory alongside one another offers a distinct view of the worlds that critical writers create and inhabit. This reading strategy also contributes to a view of composing that not only accounts for tools and technology (as so much recent work does, with great sophistication) but also those partners, not often included in theories or studies of composing, who emerge in acknowledgments—feelings, time, animals, and random material phenomena—that constitute different sorts of writing matter, leading to the distinct conclusion that all writing is radically collaborative. Acknowledgments use tactics that mix compulsory and non-compulsory debts, amounting to an implicit theory of composing that might be summed up as *writing is contamination*: created through contact with and exposure to diverse influences and agents.

23

Throughout this book, especially chapters two and three, I summon examples from contemporary academic acknowledgments published in critical books by rhetoric and composition scholars as well as by scholars beyond the field who address issues that impact and get taken up regularly in writing studies: feminism, queer theory, cultural theory, digital humanities, and more generally work across the humanities, the broad context for my study (see Appendix A for acknowledgment sources). I focus on books rather than journal articles or chapters because the former more consistently designate formal space to acknowledging, providing robust views of the genre. The books from which I've drawn span 37 years, with the earliest published in 1977 (Shaughnessy) and the most recent in 2014 (Monroe). My materials produce a selective view of acknowledgments and relationship to writing theory and practice, as I draw widely and unsystematically from texts that have been influential (i.e., Berthoff; Brodkey; Harris, *A Teaching*; Jarratt and Worsham) as well as from those that represent diverse standpoints and scholarly projects (i.e., Hawhee; Payne; Royster; Vitanza; Weaver). To a great extent, my choices bear "the traces of authorial predilection and prejudice," to borrow from John Tomlinson (73), as they include some titles on my bookshelves, others I've encountered in my research over the years, some that were recommended, titles arrived at through citations, ones I discovered while parked for hours in the PE1404 section of the library stacks, and still others I came across serendipitously (in a colleague's office, while searching online, at a used book sale, and so forth).

My choice of texts for analysis is inspired less by a cohesive mission than by circuitous reading paths through which ideas for my study began to accumulate. That is, this book favors a reading strategy that might be described as "productive wandering," a phrase coined by Jonathan Alexander, Jacqueline Rhodes, and me in "Indirection, Anxiety, and the Folds of Reading." We advocate a reading strategy that attaches "value and power" to reading "both by purposeful, guided choices as well as by accidents, associations, and sensory, felt pairings" (46). This approach is well suited to studying a non-obligatory genre that is sometimes read, other times skimmed or ignored entirely. Acknowledgments, usually written last but appearing first in a book, occupy an ambivalent status akin to the ubiquitous reflective letter in first-year composition classes. Both, unfairly or not, are characterized as perfunctory, unsurprising genres, yet both contain enormous potential to reveal something of writing's vitality. To preserve that vitality rather than codify it through a typology of sorts, my selection of texts is generally guided by an interest in writing as "a complex site for the enactment of prefaces, in which writers and texts preface each other, constantly inaugurating and deferring their own beginnings," as Anis Bawarshi puts it in his Preface to *Genre and the Invention of the Writer* (ix).

Most of the acknowledgments I read averaged three to four pages. The majority conform to the following formula, roughly organized in this general order:

- Opening statement signaling that, like every other writing project, this one benefited from insights, commentary, and advice from others.

- Listing of those others and of institutional, personal, and emotional supports along the way.

- Listing, where relevant, of venues where earlier instantiations of the work were presented, followed by thanks to groups who made those presentations possible, and permissions granted to publish chapters or excerpts of previously published works.

- Intimate thanks to close family and friends, without whom the project would not have been possible.

Despite the more-or-less common observance of genre conventions across acknowledgments, I found that writers reproduce more than clichés about networks of influence and social context. They collectively, and presumably without intent, enact a sophisticated theory of writing partnerships, which I develop in the remainder of this book.

CHAPTER ORGANIZATION

Chapter one foregrounds my interpretive stance on acknowledgments by outlining a set of composing theories sensitive to small moments, idiosyncrasies, and the flotsam of writing. The theories of composing that inform my study illuminate the everyday marginalia of writing (i.e., hands, food, telephones). The work of Mina Shaughnessy, Janet Emig, Ann Berthoff, Sondra Perl, Lisa Ede and Andrea Lunsford, Marilyn Cooper, Linda Brodkey, and Margaret Syverson asserts the marginalia of composing as worthy of study, a valuation that influences my treatment of acknowledgments—a fringe or threshold genre—as a site where authors store information about writing partnerships. Chapter one establishes acknowledgments as lens through which to study writing partners, which in this study include animals, feelings, technologies, matter, time, and materials interacting in both harmonious and antagonistic ways with writing. This chapter also unearths Emig's 1971 use of "significant other," an intriguing progenitor of my use of "partners" throughout this book. My overall purpose in chapter one is to show how theories of communal composing, as represented by the work of those theorists named above, encourage unconventional looking at writers' encounters with things and others—a baseline that anticipates my analysis in the following chapters. From here, chapters unfold by focusing on acknowledgments as a paratext that writers use to identify the following writing partners: good feeling, time, and animals.

Chapters two and three focus on good feeling and time, respectively, as writing partners that appear in acknowledgments. Both rely on textual analysis of acknowledgments drawn from a wide range of sources in and related to writing studies. Because much of my prior research focused on emotion and affect studies, I came to these texts with an already established interest in how writers would articulate the relationship between feeling and writing. Thus, as a reader and a researcher, I was attuned to those moments, predisposed to pay special attention to the emotional and physical aspects of composing. Chapter two illustrates writers' compulsions to narrate good feelings about writing in acknowledgments. Framing this compulsion as a performative feeling script, I discuss acknowledgments as pedagogical texts that teach readers and writers how to orient appropriately to writing. More specifically, this chapter reads affect and acknowledgments as partners that together form a pedagogy of how writing is supposed to feel. The final section explores the worrying consequences of projecting too much happiness onto writing, including the marginalization of writing blocks and writing differences associated with linguistic diversity as well as the valorization of writing as an able-bodied pursuit.

As a writer, I wanted to know how others endure the stillness, withstand the psychological and emotional demands, and essentially make the return to writing that I often find so difficult in my own process. Enduring, withstanding, and returning are of course temporal indicators that index the real-time labor of writing. Thus, my focus on time as a writing partner in chapter three emerges from the preceding discussion of good feeling. Feelings are rooted in time, just like everything else, and so I wanted to understand better how the affective experience of writing unfolds over time and figures into what writers select to recount in acknowledgments (itself a high intensity temporal genre that typically marks the end of a project). In addition, I have written elsewhere about time—more specifically, "slow agency"—in relation to writing program administration (WPA). Advocating for WPAs to recognize "the value of sometimes residing longer than is comfortable in the complexity, stillness, and fatigue of not knowing how to proceed," I sought to draw attention to pacing and agency within the context of administration (80). What are the costs and benefits of being in the moment as an administrator? Is it possible to embrace stillness as a legitimate philosophical basis for doing administration?

These sorts of questions find their way into my study of time and writing, where I explore a destabilized present in acknowledgments and highlight writers' efforts to chart their work in and across time. Efforts to situate writing in time reveal its incremental aspects often submerged by final products. Likewise, how writers inhabit time, an all too important and frequently stressful writing partner, is visible in acknowledgments. This chapter focuses on constructions of time in acknowledgments that reveal time "thickening," a phrase that describes time's density, the way it becomes thick with bodies, feelings, materials, and others. I'm particularly interested in understanding how writers identify time as an orienting device that gestures both to a writing past and to writing's future, a horizon of possibility. Writing's time, as it intersects with possibility, attachment, and endurance, and is articulated in acknowledgments, forms my primary focus in this chapter. Writers' accounts of time emphasize pacing schemes that deepen my study of feeling and animal companions as writing partners, the subject of chapter four.

Drawing on textual analysis and qualitative data, chapter four focuses on the role of animal partners in writing activities. This chapter addresses the idea of "withness," or the ways in which animals and humans, tangled together in everyday encounters, co-create writing experiences and spaces in large and small ways. After presenting examples from written acknowledgments that demonstrate how nonhuman creatures contribute to writing activities, I integrate the text and image results of my field research showing how writers conceive the contributions that animal companions make to their composing lives. These contributions acknowledge partners that render writing an art of living and engaging with a range of others. One major claim that emerges from the chapter is that we are entangled with others when we write, and this relationship reveals both radical asymmetry—we are indissolubly different—and powerful alignment across differences.

The conclusion proposes that writing research reveals, above all else, the beautiful mangle of practice that defines writing as an activity. In addition, I reflect on the relevance of studying paratexts—including and exceeding acknowledgments—for writing studies scholarship. Finally, the postscript threads together excerpts from acknowledgments that, much like an exquisite corpse, constitute an assemblage of parts that become something altogether different than their original referents, exceeding the intentions of individual creators. My purpose is to illustrate and enact a rhetoric of partnership that deliberately plays with subjectivity, experience, authorship, and memory, thereby dramatizing the idea that writing is a populated act impossible without others. This book is essentially an experiment in paying attention to a paratext that seems especially fertile even while consistently overlooked by scholars of writing and rhetoric, not to mention scholars in just about every other field, and scorned (but secretly and regularly read first) by readers and critics alike.

CHAPTER 1

ACKNOWLEDGING COMMUNAL COMPOSING

That acknowledgments are ambivalent sites prone to generate charges of narcissism as well as pleasurable reading detours suggests something about composing itself. A site where writing about writing is foregrounded, acknowledgments epitomize the fraught qualities of composing laid bare by critics: we want to know how writing happens, *and* knowing how it happens potentially detracts from writing's power and value. Within composition studies, how writing happens has of course been at the center of the field since at least the 1960s. The evolution of the field, particularly tensions between product and process approaches to teaching writing, might be said to mirror in some ways the opposing views of acknowledgments laid out in the previous chapter. The efficiency of product gave way to the disorder of process, a broad statement that sets the stage for the following discussion of composing as a site of study in the field.

Composing, as an activity and object of study, arguably represents the most consequential body of research in writing studies. Looking back at the infamous Dartmouth Conference of 1966, we see a contest between teachers and scholars that, in the end, gave considerable legitimacy to the process movement and consequently to the idea that composing is recursive and inventional, an act of doing rather than knowing. Prior to insights of the process movement, writing, as Janet Emig memorably put it, was presented in such a way as to suggest "no wisp or scent anywhere that composing is anything but a conscious and antiseptically efficient act" ("Uses" 48). James Britton's growth model, which positioned developmental psychology as a basis for understanding composing, proved to be enormously influential, notwithstanding critiques of the expressive emphasis and resulting neglect of the social purposes of language and composing. As Harris points out in his history of composition studies, one appreciable result of the growth model is that writing and language use more generally became central to what students learned and teachers taught (*A Teaching* 21). In effect, Dartmouth catalyzed a new pedagogical and intellectual model for English. Instead of teaching English through text consumption, achieved by reading and analyzing literary texts, Britton and his British colleagues at Dartmouth advocated teaching English through writing. Of course, this is a much truncated and simplified account (for fuller ones, see Berlin; Harris, *A Teaching*; S. Miller, *Textual*), but suitable to my purposes, for I want to emphasize that positioning composing as an activity remains a rupture point for our discipline. The shift in emphasis from consumption to production in English studies generated writing theories and practices focused on invention as well as conceptions of writing as interacting with other systems of activity, an idea central to my study.

This chapter excavates work by early influential women scholars of composing whose research anticipates my own. The groundwork laid by Mina Shaughnessy, Janet Emig, Ann Berthoff, Sondra Perl, Lisa Ede and Andrea Lunsford, Marilyn Cooper, Linda Brodkey, and Margaret Syverson has encouraged me to look attentively at writing's conditions and surround in acknowledgments by turning me toward writing and embodiment; writing as interfacing with sensory and environmental conditions; and writing partnerships. Rather than explicitly focusing on acknowledgments, this chapter establishes the theoretical groundwork necessary for understanding writing partnerships that guides my study throughout this book.

Before moving on, I want to note that I didn't set out to map exclusively female contributions to composing theory. The work had a gravitational pull on me, as it welcomed (seeming) marginalia (e.g., hands, typewriters, bundles) into discussions of composing, providing a strong foundation for my own work. For example, when Berthoff calls paragraphs "gathering hands" (218) or Emig refers to writing habits like "sharpen[ing] all pencils before writing time" (50), they coax me to fixate on small moments and stay attentive to idiosyncrasies, as composing can be extrapolated from the everyday, from ritual, and from encounters with other things, people, and environments. Because my study of acknowledgments is a study of marginalia, the companionate theories of composing that frame my analysis throughout this book, theories that assert the marginalia of composing as worthy of study, offer compelling precedent. The valuation attached to what's around composing has influenced my treatment of acknowledgments—the fringe, or threshold genre—as a site where authors store provocative and mundane information about writing partnerships that can yield insights about how and where writing happens. The theorists whose work I draw from in this chapter demonstrate that the conditions of academic writing surface through isolated examples rather than overarching narratives. This attention to the small and inconsequential details of composing provides a lesson in how and where to look for records of writing activity.

By focusing on women scholars, I see an opportunity to intervene in the politics of citation that dominate research associated with my study of writing's surround via acknowledgments: object oriented ontology, actor-network and post-process theories as well as theories of materialism more generally in composition studies. Male theorists appear with regularity—i.e., Sid Dobrin, Byron Hawke, Martin Heidegger, Thomas Kent, Bruno Latour, Paul Prior, Thomas

Rickert—without discussion of what this regularity suggests about either theory or the field. Why are distributed models of writing an overwhelmingly male domain? Where are the women who pioneered work on composing that establishes precedent for exploring these issues? For Shaughnessy, Emig, Berthoff, and Perl, in particular, research originates with students. Perhaps this has something to do with why they are not often aligned with new composing theories today. Practice is generally overshadowed by theoretical concepts in current conversations (a notable exception is Shipka's work) in an effort to develop a robust theoretical and intellectual context for writing. My feeling is that we need not sacrifice one for the other; praxis, to my mind, is what gives our field not just definition but consequence. Bringing women's contributions to the foreground is one small way to maximize consequence and to interrupt academic citation practices—really, acknowledgment practices—a modest hope for this project. With that, I set out below to describe the theoretical basis informing my use of writing partners as a vibrant concept for the study of acknowledgments.

COMPOSING COMPOSING

Mina Shaughnessy's groundbreaking *Errors and Expectations*, published in 1977, went a long way toward acknowledging composing as an activity that one can practice and refine. She argues, for example, that beginning writers often have no idea what it means to have a writing process, and instead conceive writing "as a single act, a gamble with words, rather than a deliberate process whereby meaning is crafted stage by stage" (81). Writing behavior is thus appropriate content to discuss in a composition course, in her view. Among the behaviors she describes are "idiosyncratic preferences for certain kinds of paper or pens or tables or times of day, as well as routines [writers] follow for arriving at final copy" (81). The "privacy" of writing is an impediment to beginning writers and to their willingness to trust what she calls "intellectual vibrations," or "inner promptings that generally reveal to writers where their best energies lie" (82). Shaughnessy balances writers' inner "felt thoughts" (80) with outer engagement—specifically, the value of dialogue, both with others and with oneself (82), contending that "[w]ithout these dialogues, thoughts run dry and judgment falters" (82). She also values talk because it creates a "real audience" of teacher and peers (83), which she views as crucial to writing with purpose and focus.

Shaughnessy addresses the physicality of composing, calling sentence-combining activities "finger exercises," which she relates to "piano or bar exercises in ballet . . . that must be virtually habitual before the performer is free to interpret or even execute a total composition" (77). She notes, however, that the "analogy weakens . . . when we remember that the writer is not performing someone else's composition . . . , and that he cannot therefore as easily isolate technique from meaning" (77–78). Nonetheless, rooting language practice in the body reinforces the physical and mental interchange that characterizes language-making. While a beginning writer may have absorbed complex syntactic forms, he is "'all thumbs' when he tries to get them into written form" (78). Shaughnessy envisions sentence-combining as a progressive activity through which writers learn to inhabit what she characterizes as the underground and surface of language. Equipped with this layered understanding of how sentences take form, writers are prepared to "untangle" them and proceed unobstructed toward meaning: "[T]he process sharpens [a writer's] sense of the simple sentence as the basic, subterranean form out of which surface complexity arises, and this insight gives him a strategy for untangling any sentence that goes wrong, whether simple or complex" (78). There are elements of seizure involved in composing as Shaughnessy describes it; writers "brea[k] into" sentences as one would a locked safe (78). Writing is a lively activity, a social act, and as such, pedagogy and corresponding theory should not bracket the social world that includes behaviors, habits, interlocutors, materials and, as Shaughnessy addresses in *Errors*, language differences and strong, often negative, feelings about writing (see 10–11).

Of course, before Shaughnessy's influential work was published, compositionists were already beginning to describe the social worlds of writing in sophisticated ways. In her 1964 "Uses of the Unconscious," Emig calls attention to tactile, physical, material, and tool-oriented aspects of writing, envisioning writing as a swirl of activity. For instance, she attributes writerly habits to "that part of the writing self that observes a regular schedule; that finds a room, desk, or even writing board of its own; that owns a filing cabinet; that sharpens all pencils before writing time; that does not eat lunch or take a drink before dinner; that cuts telephone wires; that faces a bland wall instead of a view of the Bay; even that orders cork lining" (50). Emig constructs the writing self as surrounded by things and ensconced in ritual, while also invested in self-imposed limits through self-denial and hermeticism. The detail that gave me pause in Emig's list is the mention of "cork lining"—does she mean cork drawer lining? If so, this seems awfully peculiar and, in that way, a testament to idiosyncratic writing habits. (Cutting telephone wires seems more fitting to a horror movie than a writing scene.)

In a later essay, Emig comments again on what writers need in order to write, focusing this time on the body's contribution to writing practices. Her 1978 essay "Hand, Eye, Brain" describes writing as a physical act by which writers have "begun to do something" (111). The essay asks what role the hand, eye, and brain play in the writing process. Reflecting timely resistance to machine writing, Emig notes that "the impersonal and uniform font of the typewriter may for some of us belie the personal nature of our first formulations. Our own language must first appear in our own script" (112). She continues, "In writing, our sense of physically creating an artifact is less than in any other mode except perhaps composing music; thus, the literal act of writing may provide some sense of carving or sculpting our statements, as in wood or stone" (112). Of course, composing a sound artifact surely involves playing instruments, physical movement (tapping feet, snapping fingers, swaying, etc.), and feeling, as when sound transports or roots you in place, putting you in touch with something that resonates in your body. Emig's castaway comment here doesn't indulge in the full potential of her own claims, but that doesn't diminish the original thinking she contributes to the field. Writing, for Emig, is an inscription and a cultural artifact, something with physical presence that results from bodily participation. It makes sense, then, that she views mediating writing through a typewriter as removing direct involvement of the body and ritual from the process, an idea that emerges in Shaughnessy's work too, as when she notes that handwriting is an extension of the self (15). As I'll address in more detail in the next section, Emig views writing as involving what she calls "significant others," and one could reasonably infer from the examples herein that the rituals, habits, and bodily involvement she identifies as central to writing have influence enough over the writing process to be considered significant others. This attention to others in the composing process represents an influential precursor to my thinking about composing partners.

The insertion of writing into worldly scenes gets more attention in Ann E. Berthoff's ambitious, contemplative textbook, *Forming/Thinking/Writing*. Rereading the book today, I easily forget that it's a textbook, for it has none of the tell-tale signs of that genre's current conventions (images, chunked text, color, wide margins, organization keyed to an outcomes-based composition course, etc.). Berthoff's writing is more philosophical and meandering than instructional, though the book has a clear pedagogical function, as she works out a process- and action-oriented theory of composing powered by verbs. Describing composing as an "organic process" that is active and always changing (229), Berthoff implores writers to look, construe, name, form, articulate, and gather. The writer is the doer, busily making things and interacting with the world while doing so. The textbook begins with a bold claim that makes clear her view of writing as a relational, immersive activity: "This book teaches a method of composing that focuses on the ways in which writing is related to everything you do when you make sense of the world" (1). She continues, "Making sense of the world is composing. It includes being puzzled, being mistaken, and then suddenly seeing things for what they probably are; making wrong—unproductive, unsatisfactory, incorrect, inaccurate—identifications and assessments and correcting them or giving them up and getting some new ones" (3–4). Berthoff comes at writing with arms wide open; there is a remarkable freedom and lift in her description. She constructs no discreet boundaries around inquiry, interpretation, description, writing, and the world. Writing is not partitioned off from other subjects and experiences; it is total immersion. Berthoff encourages non-instrumental writing that I (and probably others) would like to see more widely valued in composition studies today.

Like Shaughnessy and Emig, Berthoff addresses writing habits and partners. All three mention typewriters, calling to mind a sensory detail no longer so intimately attached to writing: the feel and sound of fingers hitting keys hard (not tapping, as most of us do today) in order to make a literal imprint, and of keys striking paper, sometimes clumping together, requiring the typist to separate and re-set them. In addition to being longstanding accompaniments to writing, typewriters, for Berthoff, are cognitive mechanisms much like handwriting or doodling:

> Some writers compose at the typewriter or the word processor
> because they can type faster than they can write and because
> they can't think consecutively until they see what they're
> saying in type or on the screen. Others write by hand be-
> cause they need to doodle; that kinetic activity acts as a kind
> of starter motor. Many writers can't start until they have the
> right pen, the right paper, the right chair, the right writing
> surface. (262)

Activity and tools assist thinking, and so writing. Though immersed in a field abuzz with cognitivism, Berthoff fixates on components of writing not located exclusively in the brain: kinetic activities, surfaces, sensory attachments, motors, tools. While she acknowledges differences in composing processes, she also generalizes from her own predilections for a productive writing environment in the form of general advice to writers: "Dogs and cats and roommates are hazards, to say nothing of strong gusts of wind and two-year-olds, but a large flat surface in a still room provides one of the best devices for getting a composition together" (266).

As we'll learn in chapter four, dogs and cats (and other creatures) function not as hazards but as important composing partners for many writers—though admittedly roommates, gusts of wind, and two-year-olds remain wildcards. The mention of non-writing influences, even if to disparage them, represents acknowledgment of the world beyond the text that is ultimately part of its production. Composing is part of the whole surround for Berthoff; throughout her book, she constructs classrooms as ecosystems that facilitate interaction with a wide variety of stimuli, objects, and experiences. The composing process, writes Berthoff, "is a continuum, an unbroken and continuing activity" (5), which suggests that composing is integrated into our daily lives in unobtrusive ways and is not set off from "ordinary" activity. Her book aims to take advantage of this fact through "assisted invitations" that evocatively immerse composing in daily life (i.e., journaling observations, writing grocery lists, etc.).

Berthoff's method for composing outlined in *Forming/Thinking/Writing* privileges chaos, wonder, and exploration as heuristics for writing and is encapsulated in her call to "cultivate a habit of 'careful disorderliness'" (243). It's not surprising, then, that she has pointed things to say about outlines as prewriting tools: "A method of composing that requires that you work out an outline before you start writing cannot possibly help you find the parts or guide you in bundling them: an outline is like a blueprint and, in the design of a building, drawing the blueprint is the final stage of the architect's work" (268). While my writing style complies with Berthoff's claim, I've worked with student writers who find outlines to be enabling starting points and bases for invention. If moving backwards through the process works for some, why deter writers from using outlines? Fewer imperatives for writing processes and practices are required at this point in the field's history; the diversity of our students and the sophistication of our research demand nothing less.

Berthoff's rejection of outlines is embedded in an architectural comparison that constructs writing as physical and structural; it produces shapes and contours, and forms habitable spaces and relationships. A "composition is a bundle of parts," we are told repeatedly (23). Extending this idea, Berthoff depicts poorly balanced paragraphs as "boxcars" because "each element is given the same weight and assumes the same shape" (232). Everywhere Berthoff speaks of gathering and shaping ideas, sentences, paragraphs. At one point, she memorably refers to a paragraph as that which "gathers like a hand" (218). The "gathering hand" has various functions:

> [T]he hand that holds a couple of eggs or tennis balls works
> differently from the hand that holds a bridle or a motorbike
> handle. When you measure out spaghetti by the handful,
> scoop up water by the handful, hold a load of books on your
> hip, knead bread, shape a stack of papers, build a sand castle,
> your hands move in different planes and with different mo-
> tions, according to the nature of the material being gathered.
> But in any case, the hand can gather because of the *opposable*
> thumb. . . . A paragraph gathers by opposing a concept and
> the elements that develop and substantiate it. (218)

To describe writing as a gathering hand with an opposable thumb is to underscore the embodied aspect of composing, emergent from her grounding claim that "[w]e're composers by virtue of being human" (5). For Berthoff, there is a meaningful connection between bodies and composing, a delightful insight to propel a first-year writing textbook! Insofar as Berthoff's motivation for writing is shaped by her passion for writing as a living art rather than by programmatic, institutional, state and federal, or assessment constraints, it reflects a radically different moment in the history of writing instruction than the one we inhabit today. The physical product of composing—a bundle of parts, a series of boxcars, a set of relationships—is paired for Berthoff with a process that has physical (as well as cognitive) components. So, for instance, she encourages writers to "develop an ear for language" through activities like reading aloud, crafting imitations, and memorizing (211).

Berthoff's awareness of the world of composing is an interesting complement to Sondra Perl's elaboration of felt sense, a bodily based sense of when writing feels right. As described in her 1980 essay "Understanding Composing," felt sense "calls forth images, words, ideas, and vague fuzzy feelings that are anchored in the writer's body. What is elicited, then, is not solely the product of a mind but of a mind alive in a living, sensing body" (365). Writing is often preceded by a "dawning awareness that something has clicked" (365). Perl is careful to note that writers do not "discover" hidden meaning but instead craft and construct it through what she calls a "process of coming-into-being" (367). During that process, we might find ourselves surprised by our writing, in much the same way that Berthoff courts surprise through her chaos heuristic, or her use of Marshall McLuhan's "allatonceness," connoting everything happening at once in composing.

In Perl's later book, *Felt Sense: Writing with the Body*, she articulates "Guidelines for Composing," available in both transcript and CD form, which walk writers through a process of paying attention to their bodies and their minds in open-ended but disciplined ways. (Berthoff likewise describes her textbook as developing a composing method that embraces uncertainty and ambiguity en route to complex thinking and writing.) Perl's approach to composing as involving emotional, cognitive, and intuitive elements relates to my study in its focus on bodily based composing partners. More generally, though, Shaughnessy, Emig, Berthoff, and Perl offer fine-grained examples of how to be attentive to composing and take nothing for granted, for presuming writing to be only what appears on the page or screen is a reduction that can too easily forget the world. Rereading work by these women alongside each other, it occurs to me that attentiveness is both method and content of their studies.

Other points of contact for my research include Lisa Ede and Andrea Lunsford's three decades of work during which they've developed theoretical and pedagogical models of collaborative writing as well as put it into practice Their work perhaps represents a common sense interpretation of "writing partners" in that they write together. Beyond the obvious, though, their challenges to dominant ideologies of authorship represent a sustained example of what it looks like to recognize writing as more than a belonging, which the academy strives to reinforce through merit, reappointment and tenure awards, among other means. In "Collaboration and Concepts of Authorship," they ask, "What might it mean . . . to acknowledge the inherently collaborative nature of dissertations and the impossibility of making a truly original contribution to knowledge? Would the sky fall if, on occasion, PhD students wrote dissertations collaboratively?" (172). The essay casts a wide net on collaboration in relation to academic hierarchies and credentialing procedures as well as legal and professional contexts regarding copyright and intellectual property. In the acknowledgments section of their article, Lunsford and Ede list the many people who helped to shape the piece, and then remark that their "citation practices relentlessly suppress such collaborative response and engagement while continuing to privilege traditional authorship" (180). Acknowledgments offer a space where writers can name otherwise invisible sources of productivity and inspiration; this is surely one aspect of their quietly subversive power in many texts.

Framing acknowledgments as a site where collaborative webs are made visible is consistent with Marilyn Cooper's 1986 proposal for considering writing "an activity through which a person is continually engaged with a variety of socially constituted systems" (367). This model of writing is distinct from contextual ones, in vogue when she was writing, in the following ways:

> In contrast [to contextualist models], an ecology of writing encompasses much more than the individual writer and her immediate context. An ecologist explores how writers interact to form systems: all the characteristics of any individual writer or piece of writing both determine and are determined by the characteristics of all the other writers and writings in the systems. An important characteristic of ecological systems is that they are inherently dynamic; though their structures and contents can be specified at a given moment, in real time they are constantly changing, limited only by parameters that are themselves subject to change over longer spans of time. (368)

Writing is capable of both responding to a situation and changing it. Her guiding metaphor to describe this interactive functionality is a web; one strand affects every other, remaking the whole (370). For Cooper, the ecological model envisions "an infinitely extended group of people who interact through writing"

(372). Margaret Syverson's 1999 study of writing as an ecological system widens interaction to include the interplay of writers, readers, texts, and environments large and small. Syverson prepares us to consider writing matter as at once encompassing and minute, complex and ordinary, situated and distributed, individualistic and embedded in "co-evolving" environments (xiv). For Syverson, "writers, readers and texts" are part of

> a larger system that includes environmental structures, such
> as pens, paper, computers, books, telephones, fax machines,
> photocopiers, printing presses, and other natural and hu-
> man-centered features, as well as other complex systems
> operating at various levels of scale, such as families, global
> economies, publishing systems, theoretical frames, academic
> disciplines, and language itself. (5; cf. Prior)

Writing is a primary activity through which we participate in the social world and composing is capaciously inclusive. These ideas are formative for me, as is the notion that the social world always participates in writing, cannot be excised no matter how much we might wish it otherwise.

A powerful expression of the writing-world dialectic appears in Linda Brodkey's 1987 study, *Academic Writing as Social Practice*, in which writing is anchored in scenes. Her work is fueled by a resistance to cognitivism (an inspiring adversary for social constructionists, as time has shown), which located writing too much in the writer's mind and not enough in the material world, and of course to modernism, to which she attributes the image of the writer in the garrett and its desultory effects on thinking about writing. Instead, she emphasizes the social function and materiality of language. To help make her point, she uses an excerpt from cultural theorist Raymond Williams' "The Tenses of the Imagination":

> I am in fact physically alone when I am writing, and I do not
> believe, taking it all in all, that my work has been less indi-
> vidual, in that defining and valuing sense, than that of others.
> Yet whenever I write I am aware of a society and of a language
> which I know are vastly larger than myself: not simply "out
> there," in a world of others, but here, in what I am engaged
> in doing: composing and relating. (Williams qtd. in Brodkey
> 414)

The world is in the scene of writing, though Brodkey's example indicates that, rather than an inescapable reality of writing, the presence of the world is cultivated through, in this case, Williams' "ability to imagine himself in the company of others even as he sits alone writing" (414). Indeed, Williams' consciousness of and ability to articulate his relationship to the world is a learned response, but the world is always in composing, whether we opt to recognize its presence or not. Developing consciousness of writing's entanglement with the world is central to Brodkey's project, for she views the purpose of "all writing research" to be "instituting writing as a social and material political practice in which writers endeavor to reconstruct society even as they shape and construct and critique their understanding of what it means to write, learn to write, teach writing, and do research on writing" (415).

SIGNIFICANT OTHERS

"Thanks, too, to Lolo the cat who continued to provide embodied and, often rather snugly, embedded desktop presence."

– Andy Clark, *Being There*

"To the many friends I haven't named, to the strangers with whom I've conversed at bus stops, in cabs, at academic conferences, and along the wild path of life, your stories, experiences, and insights regarding emotions have given me the strength to go on."

– Megan Boler, *Feeling Power*

"Without access to the excellent produce we get from local farmers, the job of writing this book would have been much harder. What would I have done without my lacinato kale? I'm not sure how orthodox it is to thank a food co-op in book acknowledgments, but being a member is an honor and I deeply appreciate the work of the farmers, suppliers, coordinators, and member-shoppers who make it run so smoothly, against all odds."

– Sarah Benesch, *Considering Emotions in*
Critical English Language Teaching

The above excerpts from acknowledgments grant access to partnerships that writers have seen fit to describe in the pages of their books. Clark's mention of his cat is not without precedent, as chapter four explores in depth, but it *is* without a correlate in writing theory and pedagogy. If animals are considered part of the scene of composing, enough to be deserving recipients of writers' gratitude when the project is complete, what can we say about this partnership beyond this particular example? For example, how can we conceive of such partnerships within research studies, teaching practices, theoretical frameworks? Likewise, how does Boler's attribution to strangers and random, unexpected events and encounters inflect composing as a partnered activity? Can randomness amount to anything of import to teachers and scholars? What about food and community food suppliers? Rather than treating these and other forthcoming examples as gratuitous, irrelevant, or divorced from writing activity, this book lingers on the writing fringe, the locale of suspected excessiveness, where the mechanics of gratitude meet everyday recognition of livelihood and sustenance, sometimes linked directly to writing activity, sometimes not. In the paratextual scene of acknowledgments, writing partners are on unusual display and have the potential to enhance existing studies of writing's communal, partnered dimensions.

Before beginning this project I was aware of research on writers in collaboration with others writ large, but I was surprised to stumble upon Emig's discussion of "significant others" in her 1971 study of writers in action, *The Composing Processes of Twelfth Graders*. If you're not looking for it, this quick reference easily escapes notice (91). Emig does not emphasize her word choice, nor do her critics or admirers; the groundbreaking aspect of the book—framing composing as an object of study and basis for research—is what's remembered, and for good reason. But Emig does offer a vocabulary for discussing composing that anticipates my project in unexpected ways. In her discussion of the "Components of the Composing Process," she includes the following within her discussion of context:

> More specifically, who the significant other in the composing process of secondary students is seems dependent upon whether the writing is school-sponsored or self-sponsored. For early self-sponsored and school-sponsored writing, when the subjects are preschool age or in elementary grades, parents and teachers seem fairly equally significant others. For school-sponsored writing in the secondary school, teachers are the most significant others, with parents occupying a very minor role except, occasionally, when they themselves are teachers. For self-sponsored writing among adolescent writers, particularly the able ones, the significant others are peers who also write. (92)

Emig concludes that writing in secondary schools is too other-directed, particularly too teacher-directed, and is likely a direct result of the lack of writing that secondary teachers do themselves, which she presumes leads to an oversimplification of how the composing process is taught (she later notes that she was too hard on teachers in her conclusions (see *Web* 62)).

Upon rereading this passage, I stumbled over "significant other," completely undetected in my previous readings and teachings of this text. Emig offers no explanation of how she's using that term. Some initial research as well as a check of the *OED* led me to few references during the period when she was writing. Harry Stack Sullivan's *Conceptions of Modern Psychiatry*, published in 1947, is credited with introducing the term, and his later book, *The Interpersonal Theory of Psychiatry*, published in 1953, further elaborates its significance. For Sullivan, "significant other" referenced "those who directly socialize the person to whom they are significant" (Owens). His understanding of the term emerged from his research on schizophrenia, the onset of which he traced "to unsuccessful interpersonal relationships with significant others during childhood" (Owens). Thus, a significant other was not initially defined in terms of a romantic relationship, as is common today, but designated "those persons who are of sufficient importance in an individual's life to affect the individual's emotions, behavior, and sense of self" (Owens).

Sullivan (along with social psychologist George Herbert Mead) suggests that socialization hinges on whether others view you as important. This seems consistent with Emig's usage of "significant other" in the above passage. Also likely relevant was Joseph Woelfel and Archibald Haller's "Significant Others, the Self-Reflexive Act and the Attitude Formation Process," published in *American Sociological Review* in February of 1971, the same year that Emig's book was published. It's unlikely that she read it, but perhaps the ideas were in the air, as often happened in a slower paced publishing environment. In their sociological study, Woelfel and Haller define significant others as "those persons who exercise major influence over the attitudes of individuals" (75; emphasis in original). "Attitudes" are for them "relationships between a person and an object or set of objects" (75).

The use of significant other to indicate influence is consistent with Emig's and is an evocative progenitor of "partners" in this study. Influence does not exactly match how I use partners in this study, but it does have some bearing. Influence usually evokes effects, direct and indirect power over and affect. And intriguingly, influence derives from the Latin *influentia*, meaning "to flow in." The first definition of influence in the *OED* reads, "The action or fact of flowing in; inflowing, inflow, influx: said of the action of water and other fluids, and of immaterial things conceived of as flowing in." Influence flows in and infuses, bereft of hard boundaries and clear start and end points. This idea captures very well the curatorial, distributed, and immersive characteristics of writing made visible in acknowledgments. What flows in can't be stopped, represents an agency that exceeds human involvement, and might suggest being overwhelmed or overcome by forces outside the self. Indeed, this latter implication emerges in the *OED*'s fifth definition of the term: "The capacity or faculty of producing effects by insensible or invisible means, without the employment of material force, or the exercise of formal authority . . . ascendancy, sway, control, or authority, not formally or overtly expressed."

Agents that lack overt sway over composing have emerged as significant to scholarship on ubiquitous technologies like paper, calling attention to the production and consumption of material writing partners that otherwise seem to have no intent or whose presence is simply taken for granted. Catherine Prendergast and Roman Ličko contrast paper consumption in an American university and a Slovakian one, revealing how, at the former, faculty expect paper to be widely available yet fail to realize how costly it is (her department spent $11,424 on paper during 2007–2008) (204). In Slovakia, however, the scarcity of paper and minimal access to a photocopier make plainly evident paper's expense and identity as a central technology of writing. English department faculty are allotted 70 copies per academic year, and those copies are limited to exams. The authors note that "Roman, with 60–75 students in one course, is hardpressed to adhere to the 70-photocopies a month limit, even if only for exams. In order to fit his exam into the limit, he narrows margins, chooses small font sizes, and worries about the resulting legibility" (205; cf. Mortensen).

In a similar vein, A. Suresh Canagarajah describes the conditions that framed academic research in the 1980s in his home country, Sri Lanka, explaining that paper was hard to come by so he and his colleagues used recycled pamphlets. Revision, in these circumstances, "depended on the amount of paper one could find" (*Geopolitics* 9). Since electronic and postal communication were also severely limited, they frequently learned of new developments in their fields, new books, or announcements of fellowships or conferences after the fact, limiting their ability to participate in contemporary conversations. In his own research on periphery scholars, Canagarajah faced such extreme circumstances as when an interview with a research participant was cancelled because "of a bombing raid or some other emergency" (14). In another example, he describes writing by kerosene-fueled lamps in the absence of electricity.

Shifting from environmental partners to those of form, John Trimbur and Karen Press focus on the page. Far from an empty site of inscription, a page is "active and alive, with its own invisible understructures and semiotic potentialities" (93). A written page, they explain, consists of "material forms, such as the type and quality of paper and ink in use; its own conventions, such as the rhetoric of transparency and the grid as an underlying compositional matrix; and the labor of composing pages through the available means of production, which change over time" (95–96). This argument is consistent with Trimbur's earlier discussion of delivery as a neglected rhetorical canon, which he believes "has led writing teachers to equate the activity of composing with writing itself and to miss altogether the complex delivery systems through which writing circulates" ("Composition" 189–90; cf. Ridolfo and DeVoss). All of these authors highlight the materials of writing—very real writing partners. In order to make something, we need materials that are themselves endowed with energy and agency, contributing to the final product in non-trivial ways. Without a page (screen, tablet, scroll, wall, etc.) as a surface of inscription, for example, what is writing? How would it present? The line of thought developed here operates as a thinking-partner for my effort to shift attention to companionate partners, in addition to tools and forms, as writing essentials.

Writing partners, as made visible in acknowledgments, exert indirect, seemingly immaterial, often invisible influence over writing; and sometimes thinking partners surprise, taking the lead and directing attention in unforeseen ways. Partners of all sorts overtake writing, with or without conscious awareness, and contribute to its creation. This point was reiterated for me when I recently read David Bartholomae's "Living in Style," the lead essay in his collection, *Writing on the Margins*. He begins by noting that he has always kept a commonplace book in which he includes passages from his reading and teaching that represent "striking eloquence" (1). In addition to functioning as a storehouse for what catches his attention, these passages "serve as points of reference to individual performances and positions in a larger field of ideas or debate" (1). In "Against the Grain," Bartholomae says more about the presence of others while writing:

> I feel a sense of historic moment when I write—not that I'm making history, but that I am intruding upon or taking my turn in a conversation others have begun before me. I feel a sense of the *priority of others*. Some of them, I think, are great writers, some of them are my colleagues and contemporaries, some of them are my teachers, some of them are strangers or students. . . . When I write I find I am appropriating authority from others while trying to assert my own. This is the dialectic that I feel when I write and that shapes what I do when I put words on a page. (20–21; emphasis added)

What is most important—takes precedence—are others, rather than, say, ideas, inspiration, or purpose (all of which, for Bartholomae, are inflected by others). In place of a relational model, in which various materials and agents interact to produce writing, Bartholomae depicts his writing process in terms of more and less powerful affordances. In other words, all contributors/partners are not equal. With Stacy Alaimo and Susan Hekman, my thinking throughout this book is shaped by materialist concepts of agency that "account for myriad 'intra-actions' between phenomena that are material, discursive, human, more-than-human, corporeal, and technological" (5), and yet I sometimes find the minimized role of power variables inherent in such descriptions to be inexact and, at worst, potentially dangerous when applied to analyses of oppression, trauma, and systematic violence. Thus, Bartholomae's description serves as a useful reminder that partners are not neutral. This point sometimes gets lost in materialist descriptions of assemblages that rely heavily on unweighted relationality. We can become dependent on certain partners in ways that aren't wholly enabling, that constrain productivity and entrap us in unworkable situations. Bartholomae's example is definitively not an example of the latter; rather, his emphasis on priority while writing highlights for me the larger stakes in presuming a benign relationality.

Donna Haraway emphasizes this point in her articulation of *significant otherness*, which she defines as involving "non-harmonious agencies and ways of living . . . accountable both to their disparate inherited histories and to their barely possible but absolutely necessary joint futures" (*Companion* 7; emphasis in original). When I invoke writing partners, then, I have in mind animals, feelings, technologies, matter, time, and materials interacting in both harmonious and antagonistic ways. My thinking is shaped by material feminist reconfigurations of agency. Feminists have rethought corporeality to acknowledge the mingling together of human and nonhuman matter, setting the groundwork for understanding identity as never entirely divorced from environment, medicine, science, toxins, and so forth. This view creates a case for distributed agency and for intersections with nature and environment, long a troubling pairing for feminism because of women's longstanding vexed relation to Nature. One of the main points that emerges from material feminist research is that all forms of matter, living and non-living, are significant to sociocultural, political, as well as biological systems. Applying these ideas to writing has the potential to help us describe writing practices with vibrant awareness of all that writing entails and signifies. Writers are not autonomous. Bruno Latour articulates a broader, related point in a recent article: "To be a subject is not to act autonomously in front of an objective background, but to share agency with other subjects that have also lost their autonomy" (5).

A striking example of linked agency appears in Nicholas Carr's *The Shallows: What the Internet is Doing to Our Brains*. He discusses the desperate, ailing Friedrich Nietzsche who, in 1882, after struggling with failing vision that threatened his continued writing, ordered the world's first commercially produced typewriter, the Malling-Hansen Writing Ball. Carr describes the enormous difference the Writing Ball made in Nietzsche's writing life:

> The writing ball rescued Nietzsche, at least for a time. Once
> he had learned touch typing, he was able to write with his

eyes closed, using only the tips of his fingers. Words could pass from his mind to the page. He was so taken with Malling-Hansen's creation that he typed up a little ode to it:

> The writing ball is a thing like me: made of iron
>
> Yet easily twisted on journeys.
>
> Patience and tact are required in abundance,
>
> As well as fine fingers, to use us.

In March, a Berlin newspaper reported that Nietzsche "feels better than ever" and, thanks to his typewriter, "has resumed his writing activities."

But the device had a subtler effect on his work. One of Nietzsche's closest friends, the writer and composer Heinrich Koselitz, noticed a change in the style of his writing. Nietzsche's prose had become tighter, more telegraphic. There was a new forcefulness to it, too, as though the machine's power—it's "iron"—was, through some mysterious metaphysical mechanism, being transferred into the words it pressed into the page. "Perhaps you will through this instrument even take to a new idiom," Koselitz wrote in a letter, noting that, in his own work, "my 'thoughts' in music and language often depend on the quality of pen and paper."

"You are right," Nietzsche replied. "Our Writing equipment takes part in the forming of our thoughts." (18–19)

The sensory elements of writing, relayed through description of Nietzsche's closed eyes and fingertips, in addition to the philosopher's depiction of the typewriter as a "thing like me," offers a robust intermingling of writing agents. This relationship between equipment and thinking is hardly evoked by Carr's assertion that words "could pass from his mind to the page," which suggests an osmosis-like process through which words are "passed" effortlessly. If anything, the account, particularly Koselitz's observations, emphasizes the effort exerted by Nietzsche in order to produce writing, and the role of the machine in not only production but also the "forming of our thoughts."

This final image of the writer collaborating with tools provides an apt reminder of what I have sought to accentuate in this chapter: theories of communal composing encourage unconventional looking at writers' encounters with things and others. And, as subsequent chapters illustrate, acknowledgments are a rich site for such looking, as they draw attention to subterranean aspects of composing, including a diversity of writing partners. Chapter two develops this claim by focusing on good feeling as a writing partner that has a distinct presence and function in acknowledgments. I'm interested not only in how writers use acknowledgments to archive good feelings but also in the effects of this use on conceptions of writing that influence theory and pedagogy.

CHAPTER 2
ACKNOWLEDGING GOOD FEELINGS

> "All writing . . . has the feature that it is difficult, lonely work, and satisfying mainly when finished. I face writing with enthusiasm when I am rolling the topic around in my mind . . . and I enjoy the attendant research, but I genuinely dread the moment when I have to put pen to paper—or for that matter, put fingers on the keyboard in front of the green screen."
>
> – Louis T. Milic, "How a Stylistician Writes"

Writing is ubiquitous, particularly as tools for producing it continue to proliferate beyond the "green screen" that Milic references in 1985. And experiencing a spectrum of emotions during the process of writing—from excitement to dread and back again—is arguably pervasive as well. The inner involvement of writing can sometimes make us outwardly half-present. Those closest to us are most likely to endure the divided attention and preoccupied conversations that inevitably pepper our daily lives while we are in the midst of writing projects. They are also among those most likely to know something about the dry spells, blocks, insecurities, and feelings of hopelessness likely to plague any writer at one time or another. Writing is embedded in personal life, has been known to wreck relationships and trigger unhealthy habits, just as it may strengthen bonds of appreciation and gratitude for all that is *not writing*. It's as if immersion in writing creates beer goggles: once the writing is over, the world appears promising and full of possibility, at least for a time, contrasted with the quicksand-like reality of writing in progress, which often feels like descending lower and lower into uncertainty with no clear way out or up. This dark narrative about writing is one that I feel and hear from other writers, but it's (mostly) not one I've encountered in written acknowledgments, though it is gestured toward via thanks to a friend, colleague, or family member who stood by when times got tough. The dread depicted so vividly by Milic tends *not* to be what preoccupies the genre of acknowledgments, suggesting that, when it counts, writers have blessedly short memories. Derrida's summary of the *Phaedrus* is relevant here: "writing is at once mnemotechnique and the power of forgetting" (24).

Maybe it is forgetting which accounts for the optimistic tendencies of writing about writing that are so common in acknowledgments. Barbara Ehrenreich describes optimism as a "cognitive stance, a conscious expectation, which presumably anyone can develop through practice" (4). This stance is likely learned by exposure to existing examples, as I believe to be the case with acknowledgments. Optimism and its positivity can point us in specific directions, most obviously toward objects of these expressions. They can also lead us to certain kinds of scripts for living that substitute idealized versions of reality for less than ideal ones. For example, admonitions to "go green" issue imperatives (much like "just do it" and "just say no") to emphasize the importance of individual choices and reassure us that "going green" is possible in an industrialized country. Awareness of the organized, systemic degradation of the earth might end up debilitating people, making us feel as if choosing a reusable bag, for example, is utterly absurd in the face of wide-scale environmental destruction. The promise of "go green" is that a clean, smart, contained, and conscious way of living is within reach and offers its own distinct rewards. The slogan, in other words, is a performative; its articulation is also its action and its promise.

Also performative, writing about writing in acknowledgments tends toward a largely positive, cheerful, funny, harmonious, appreciative, warm and loving discourse of resilience—exactly the sort of qualities one would want to associate with writing (the sprawling self-help industry around writing frames this want in plain economic terms). Positivity associated with writing forms an ideology, "the way we explain the world and think we ought to function within it" (Ehrenreich 4), that no doubt obscures, even wills away, writing difficulties, blocks, and failures. Via acknowledgments, writers might be thought of as ideologues, spokespersons on behalf of writing as good feeling. One wonders if, by always showcasing the healthy and productive elements of writing, we lose touch with fuller depictions, and if losing touch is ultimately the real purpose of acknowledgments. If we were to find, rather than lose, touch, after all, we might say something similar to C.H. Knoblauch, who remarks that, while he sometimes enjoys writing, he also finds that it

> frequently gives me both a headache and a backache, just as
> the jackhammer does, I imagine, when a worker has spent
> all day vibrating over it. Worse, writing causes endless anxi-
> ety about that most dreaded of academic catastrophes—the
> saying of something indefensibly dumb in print, where it can-
> not be denied, disowned, or restated as though it had never
> happened. (134)

Knoblauch's anxiety about reception is echoed by Elspeth Probyn, who contends that the "specter of not interesting readers and the constant worry about adequately conveying the interest of our chosen topics" contributes to what she calls a "shame-induced ethics of writing" (89). For Probyn, shame can productively influence writing because it is "a visceral reminder to be true to interest, to be honest about why or how certain things are of interest" (73).

Of course, shame and other self-assessment affects related to writing are not always experienced as generative. Some may contribute to serious blocking. Mike Rose presents a portrait of blocked writers in his preface to *When a Writer Can't Write*, illustrating how anxiety and other issues can create formidable obstacles to writing:

> Thoughts won't come, and when they do they evanesce as
> the writer tries to work them into written language. Pauses
> become longer and longer and transmogrify into avoidances.
> Inner conflicts manifest themselves in jumbled syntax and
> unclear diction. The demands of one's life and the ways one
> has been taught to deal with them interfere again and again
> with writing. . . . And so goes the painful litany. (ix)

In sharp contrast, acknowledgments are largely bereft of writing pain, whether productive or destructive, indicating that this genre is more aspirational than descriptive. Acknowledgments serve multiple purposes for writers and readers: they do the obvious in terms of formalizing methods of thanking people, institutions, and others who enabled a writing project; provide a public forum for writers to pay psychic, intellectual, and emotional debts; and offer release after completion of a significant piece. Also, as I'll discuss below, they serve as an unofficial archive of good feelings that writers would like to associate with writing, a drive no doubt inspired by the afterglow of completion. Acknowledgments, that is, are not more revealing than the rest of an academic book. They are a different class of performatives, offering clues toward understanding what writing involves, needs, consumes, desires.

Borrowing from Sara Ahmed's formulation of happy feelings in *The Promise of Happiness*, this chapter postulates that the abundance of good feeling in acknowledgments functions as an affective script, a good feeling partner. This script associates writing with good feeling, or the "right" feelings about writing. Ahmed, interested in how happiness functions as a coercive promise directing us toward certain life choices and away from others, focuses on figures who challenge happiness imperatives: feminist killjoys, melancholic migrants, unhappy queers, and angry black women. Happiness, for her, "involves a way of being aligned with others, of facing the right way" (45). While the reproduction of good feelings attached to writing obviously is on a different order and pain-scale than happiness imperatives associated with compulsory heterosexuality, Ahmed's ideas make it possible to consider good feelings as performatives aimed at associating writing with a good. In this sense, acknowledgments are oftentimes archives of good feeling, storage for positive associations with writing that seek to proliferate goodness. Good feelings in acknowledgments describe "not only what we are inclined toward . . . but also what we should be inclined toward" (Ahmed, *Promise* 199). When they include more than a list of permissions or boilerplate thank-yous to funding sources, acknowledgments are pedagogical: they teach readers and potential writers how to orient appropriately to writing. This chapter reads affect and acknowledgments as partners that together form a pedagogy of how writing is supposed to feel. I then explore the worrying consequences of projecting too much happiness onto writing, including the marginalization of writing blocks and of writing differences associated with linguistic diversity as well as the valorization of writing as an able-bodied pursuit.

In this chapter and the next one, I rely on textual analysis of acknowledgments excerpted from a wide range of sources in and related to writing studies. Of the 75 books referenced throughout this study, all made mention of what I interpreted as either "good feeling" or "time," the latter of which I'll address in the next chapter. Weaving together excerpts from nearly 20 acknowledgments, this chapter interprets as "good feeling" references to laughter; comfort and support from family, friends, home, music, and objects; positive emotions (joy, love, happiness), and physical activity.

GOOD FEELING

What we learn from acknowledgments is that writing is supposed to be—and, when successful, often *is*—pleasurable for writers; good feelings are supposed to cohere around it and bad ones, if writing guides and self-help texts are any indication, are to be overcome through practical strategies and writing rules (i.e., Fowler; Strausser; Yagoda). Within composition studies, a field dedicated to studies of writing, rhetoric, and pedagogy, the disassociation of writing from bad feelings might help explain the limited research on writer's block. Keith Hjortshoj notes that blocking is widely misunderstood in academia and in the culture generally, leading to responses that treat writing as more of a mechanical matter than a holistic art. Blocked academic writers in his study describe themselves as feeling "*immobilized, motionless, stuck, stranded, mired, derailed, disengaged, disembodied, paralyzed,* or *numb*," revealing that blocks are more than cognitive difficulties; they are experienced mentally and physically (9). "Somewhere in the process of doing something they want and need to do, and are fully capable of doing," writes Hjortshoj, "these writers run into trouble they shouldn't have" (9). In other words, nothing is ostensibly stopping them from writing; they are capable, smart, and have the resources and tools to write. Blocked writers, however, challenge imperatives to feel good about writing, confounding advice modalities and calling to mind a point Ahmed makes about unhappiness that might just as well apply here: "I think what is underestimated by affirmative ethics is the *difficulty* of giving our attention to—and sustaining our attention on—certain forms of suffering" (216).

This point became very clear to me when I read acknowledgments that refuse good feelings. In 2012, I served as a reader for a dissertation, entitled *Emotional Literacy and the Challenge of ESL Academic Literacy*. The study by Joseph Slick develops grounds for an explicitly emotional discourse about second-language learners' experiences of writing. Reading the opening pages of his acknowledgments, I was not prepared to encounter his direct, unapologetic bad feelings about writing:

> I could not have survived without [my wife's] support to continue this lonely and depressing endeavor. The dissertation challenges a dissertator to be resilient in the face of the "symbolic violence" of the dissertation, and I could not have survived without her love. She has taught me that a dissertation is not the ends to a successful life, but a means to understand how to handle the difficulties in life. That includes how to plan and prepare to meet the unexpected challenges that are always lying just around the corner. . . . Most of all, this dissertation was a lesson in how to survive and overcome obstacles. A completed dissertation hides the sadness, the tears, the frustration and the depression of the dissertation process. (v-vi)

Slick knows the conventions and expectations of acknowledgments—he discussed them during the defense—but he wanted to express his truth about the dissertation process. And his truth was hard, lonely, heart-breaking, dark, depressing. His language can be read as a refusal to consent to good feeling and its circulation in the economy of writing frequently anticipated in acknowledgments. Slick doesn't hold in place a positive conception of writing, softened by the increasing fuzziness of the rearview mirror.

Slick is an outlier in this regard, an "affect alien . . . one who converts good feelings into bad" (Ahmed, *Promise* 49). The feelings typically deposited in acknowledgments stir good feelings and create writing worlds nourished by love and care that, wittingly or not, obscure the many challenges to writing. One manifestation of good feelings comes through writers' frequent praise of the emotional environment developed by family members, often represented as the backbone of writing progress. Constance Weaver, for example, notes that her son and partner both offered "unfailing support for my work and [brought] joy to my daily life" (xiv). Victor Villanueva, writing of his wife's importance, confides that from her he knows "of magic, of loving. And knowing love opens up possibilities, allows one to be utopian in the midst of all that sometimes seems hopeless" (ix).

Ann Cvetkovich likewise writes in euphoric terms about the role her partner has played in her life: "And then there's Gretchen Phillips, who for over ten years now has loved me passionately and extravagantly. In her perpetual insistence that I follow my heart's desire, she has helped me remember that writing can be a labor of love, and she has given me a constant supply of reasons to love her back" (xi). In another outpouring of affection, Paul Prior confides the following:

> Over the last ten years, Nora and Anna have illuminated my days
> (and often my nights) with their love, joys, and sorrows, and
> insights that continue to teach me much about life. Finally, for
> 22 years, Julie Hengst has been my full partner in all spheres of
> activity. In addition to remarkable moral and material support,
> she has contributed to my thinking in general and to this specific
> text in innumerable substantive ways, only hinted at by the dis-
> cussion in chapter 10 of the influence of her research. (xviii)

Christina Haas is less specific about the contributions of family members but attributes a productive emotional scene for writing partly to her daughters, whom she describes as "studies in strength, determination, and force of will, and there were many days when I looked to them for example. They also provided hugs at critical times" (xvii). She goes on to thank two women and their staff "for the unwavering support they provided to my family; their efforts continue to allow me to manage a life of work and family on a day-to-day basis" (xvii). Margaret Syverson, author of *The Wealth of Reality*, notes that she has "been nourished by the love, encouragement, and strength I have received from my family and extended family, the real wealth of my reality . . ." (xxi).

Others thank family for helping to prioritize what's most important. In this category, Nedra Reynolds writes, "This book has been written in a loving home and has made me appreciate more than ever the joys of placemaking. Truman and Bentley [presumably, pets] faithfully follow me up to my study, and Martin keeps all kinds of things growing around here, including me" (xii). And Shari Stenberg credits her husband with keeping her tuned in to her own life. Specifically, his "patience, perspective, and love not only guide me, but also remind me of what matters most" (x). Shipka thanks others for keeping her company and "perhaps more importantly, for pulling me away from the process every now and then, and providing me with something else to focus on, respond to, and care about" (xiii). Reynolds' ability to "appreciate more than ever" the pleasures of home, Stenberg's to remember "what matters most," and Shipka's to discover "something else to . . . care about" indicate that writing competes in a world always threatening to consume the writer, distance her from all other matter(s), and cause her to forget the small pleasures and the vitality of others as directly and indirectly important to writing and writer. In a way, these acknowledgments might serve as an indirect response to David Bartholomae's musing in "Against the Grain" regarding the difficulty of writing: "Writing gets in my way and makes my life difficult, difficult enough that I sometimes wonder why I went into this business in the first place. There is work that comes easier to me" (20). The writers above seem to invert this logic by suggesting that writing, in essence, magnifies the importance of all that is not writing. Writing and not writing, in other words, are inseparable complements to one another.

Familiar "not writing" complements that contribute to writing success are often bodily based. Laughter, for example, emerges as a significant part of the emotional scenery of writing, one that especially emphasizes the importance of withness. Krista Ratcliffe thanks her family "for supporting me with their patience, love, and laughter" (xiv). Kirsch thanks her partner for "years of friendship, love, and laughter" (Kirsch and Rohan xii); Sondra Perl notes that her editor/friend kept her "laughing as well as writing." Ahmed, in *On Being Included*, expresses appreciation of her partner, "whose questions keep me thinking and whose jokes (good and bad!) keep me laughing" (x). Harris, in *Rewriting*, notes that he was "buoyed, as always, by the warmth, laughter, affectionate irreverence, and good company of my wife . . . and my daughters . . ." (136). Kathleen Stewart names three figures nearby during the completion of her book who have "spun around the thing, day to day, with grace, squeals of laughter and rage, rolled eyes, whispers, headaches, distractions, interruptions, and smiling eyes (or knowing smirks)" (x). Laughing and appreciating others' laughter signal the body in repose, a physical release or catharsis. Laughing often means letting down your guard and allowing yourself to be caught up in moments of surprise or unpredictability without worry. Laughter creates concerted efforts to break silence. Laughter can also function to build community by highlighting common ground even as differences remain intact.

Laughter, like much else that gets mentioned in acknowledgments, is often anchored in domestic scenes that support sustainable writing habits. Notably, the inevitable annoyances and frustrations, or more extreme forms of unpleasantness familiar to domesticity, go unmentioned. This is perhaps an apt example of how the reproduction of good feeling forms a writing economy. Ahmed offers a useful explanation of this point:

> The expressions can be repeated by others, as a form of return, which will affect what impressions we have of that space. Expressing bad feeling can even become habitual in certain times and places, as a way of belonging to an affective community. The use of complaint as a form of social bonding would be a case in point. Good feelings are also affective. . . . Smiling,

> laughing, expressing optimism about what is possible will
> affect others. It is not that you necessarily catch the feeling
> but that the experience of being with and around a person
> in a good mood gives a certain lightness, humor, and energy
> to shared spaces, which can make those spaces into happy
> objects, what we direct good feelings toward. (*Promise* 43)

Likewise, reading acknowledgments may not change your disposition toward writing, but the experience of reading others' positive accounts of writing may help you accumulate your own storehouse of good feelings. This would explain why writers "direct good feelings toward" acknowledgments, reproducing the affects they've become accustomed to encountering there. Holding bad affect at bay and treating acknowledgments as spaces where writing as good feeling surfaces represent forms of emotion management aimed at maintaining appropriate social norms. Good feelings in acknowledgments, like happiness generally, involve "the comfort of repetition, of following lines that have already been given in advance" (Ahmed 48).

In composition studies, those lines often lead right to students. Jody Shipka literalizes this by addressing her students directly in the acknowledgments of her book:

> Your work challenged and amazed me then and continues, all
> these years later, to challenge and amaze me. Collectively and
> individually, you have taught me so very much about po-
> tentials for meaning, for composing texts and lives, in short,
> for thinking more about what it might take to work toward
> a composition (or compositions) made whole. For all that,
> and for your willingness to allow me to share your work with
> others, I am most grateful. (xii)

Less effusive and not stated in direct address, Shari Stenberg puts the matter simply: "My students are an endless resource of energy and inspiration" (ix).

On the one hand, these kinds of thanks are so routine in the genre that they barely merit attention. On the other, they reveal the important role that acknowledgments play as storage for good feelings and their habitual production, cultivating the impressions of and objections to acknowledgments outlined in the introduction. Impressions, in my usage here, are uses of language that press, as an actual machine press does, changing the shape of something through the application of pressure to make an imprint. When acknowledgments are treated as texts that make imprints, they exceed their marginal status. They constitute near imperatives to like writing and to express attunement with all that touches writing, understanding "touch" to include what presses on writing from the outside—another word for this might be contaminants. Acknowledgments are a powerful record of writing's impurities, its contaminated dealings with whatever and whoever it comes in contact.

Another way to think about contamination—or the mingling of forces and energies in writing environments—is through the framework of partnerships. Acknowledgments house a record of partnerships that have real affective value to writing environments. It's not that they prove there's no subject who writes, which strikes me as utterly absurd as I sit here writing for days on end, feeling the physical aches of being stationary too long and the mental exhaustion of pushing forward despite a desire to stop and do something, anything else (I'm writing before a window that overlooks a blue sky dotted with puffy white clouds . . .). Thus, evacuating the subject will not produce a more authoritative, rigorous theory of writing, as some postprocess theories suggest (e.g., Dobrin, Rice, Vastola), nor would this move be relevant to my students or myself. We are writing; there's no way around that. Rather, acknowledgments illustrate that the writer depends on and benefits from all kinds of assistance and support delivered through a variety of sources. Through acknowledgments, writers position themselves within a web of others whose ultimate invisibility in the final product distorts how a work comes together, creating an impression of writing as seamless, linear, untroubled. Pages turn, screens scroll, words follow words—these assurances can obscure what happened to make language into something.

The next section discusses good feeling entwined with sensory experiences and physical movement, common writing partners in acknowledgments. Working both with examples from acknowledgments and from essays in which writers discuss their writing practices, these examples give a different resonance to "good" than does the foregoing discussion. In part, what's different is that scenes of writing associated with good feeling are explicitly articulated as embodied—and, moreso as the foregoing examples indicate, able-bodied.

ALL OF YOUR SENSES

"[W]riting is to be done by the feel, for it is a tacit craft."
 – Richard Lloyd-Jones, "Playing for Mortal Stakes"

In a *Paris Review* interview, novelist Haruki Murakami comments that music is an important writing partner for him. "I've been listening to jazz since I was thirteen or fourteen years old," he explains. "Music is a very strong influence: the chords, the melodies, the rhythm, the feeling of the blues are helpful when

I write. I wanted to be a musician, but I couldn't play the instruments very well, so I became a writer. Writing a book is just like playing music: first I play the theme, then I improvise, then there is a conclusion, of a kind" ("The Art"). Noted theorist Slavoj Žižek similarly describes music as central to his work: "I cannot survive without music; I always work with music, with loud music. I cannot survive without five or six hours of chamber music per day" (Olson 198–99). Žižek, like Slick, who "could not survive without [his wife's] love," uses a language of urgency, framing writing partners in terms of survival. The codependency between writers and their others, whatever form they take, inspires awareness of writing as a needy, vulnerable, difficult process—something that one *survives* thanks to companionate others.

The pairing of writing and music is crucial for me as well, as I presume it is for many other writers. Writing, much like running, has a pace established by the music I'm playing. If I want to write quickly, without concern for particulars, I'll play fast-paced tracks; if I want to edit or revise, lingering longer on what I've produced, I might play a moody, slower selection that creates a hypnotic focus. (Runners can use apps to create playlists that correspond to a desired pace; not a bad idea for writers.) Music and writing often generate creative energy, as is the case for Ann Cvetkovich, who begins *An Archive of Feeling* with a discussion of queer feminist punk band Le Tigre. Citing "Keep on Livin'," a song about survival after sexual trauma, Cvetkovich explains how the band functions as a partner in her efforts to articulate the purpose of her book: "Sometimes the most effective way I can explain my project is to point to work like theirs because it articulates better than I can what I want to say. If I were to 'follow the trail of breadcrumbs in my head' (to quote Kathleen Hanna) and try to tell the story of how I came to write this book, I would probably start not with trauma but with depression" (1–2). The band's work, and especially that song, serve as focal points that help bring Cvetkovich's project into being; more than scenery or aesthetic touchstone, Le Tigre is an essential contaminant in the book's making.

In his acknowledgments, anthropologist Tim Ingold goes further, describing his cello as "truly a co-author" of his book *Being Alive*. The cello, he writes, has "become so much a part of me and of the way I am that when I think and write, it thinks and writes in me" (xiv). The creative energy formed by this partnership indicates the indelible role of sensory things and of objects in composing. Ingold's cello would qualify as what Sherry Turkle calls an "evocative object"— objects as life companions that spin worlds, combining intellect, feeling, and creativity (5). In some cases, Turkle notes, we "feel at one with our objects" (9). This certainly seems to describe Ingold's relation to the cello; there is no distinction between self and cello when it comes to writing. They are mutually enabling and sustaining extensions of one another.

More evidence of writing's holistic character is available through the frequent mention of physical activity and writing. Lynn Bloom, in "How I Write," explains that "After a slow start in the morning, my energy, ability to concentrate, and creativity build throughout the day and evening, with time out for meals, an occasional nap, and an invigorating evening swim" (36). Murakami is forthcoming about acknowledging physical movement and sensory factors in his writing process (though he doesn't name these factors as such), particularly in contrast to describing the role of other people—mentors, influences, trusted readers, and so forth—in his writing life. In fact, in *The Paris Review* interview, Murakami describes himself as a loner with no discernible community of writers. Claiming that he has no writer-friends in Japan, he describes the awkward embarrassment he feels around other writers when in the U.S.: "At Princeton, there was a luncheonette, or something like that, and I was invited to eat there. Joyce Carol Oates was there and Toni Morrison was there and I was so afraid, I couldn't eat anything at all!" ("The Art"). He develops writing rituals that combine intellectual, physical, and what might be considered spiritual activities: "When I'm in writing mode for a novel, I get up at four a.m. and work for five to six hours. In the afternoon, I run for ten kilometers or swim for fifteen hundred meters (or do both), then I read a bit and listen to some music. I go to bed at nine p.m. I keep to this routine every day without variation." This extraordinary discipline and commitment to repetition is fascinating for many reasons, not the least of which is that Murakami's routine includes various sensory experiences: writing, running, swimming, reading, listening, and sleeping. His approach seems downright monastic in its simplicity as well as fetishistically balanced and healthy.

The interactive relationship between physicality and writing is frequently depicted in acknowledgments, creating a portrait of writing as inseparable from other worlds of activity, thriving in interaction, helping to create a portrait of writing as in medias res rather than as a discrete activity cut off from the natural and material world. Perl comments that her work on *Felt Sense* was "enriched by a week-long writing retreat in a farmhouse in southern Vermont where Nancy Gerson, Nancy Sommers, Mimi Schwartz, and I mixed writing with running, swimming, and cooking" (xi). Knowing this gives me a greater appreciation for her description of felt sense. The environment, composed of other writers and physical activity, seems the perfect incubator for approaching writing as perceptual, sensory, inchoate, and cognitively as well as bodily experienced.

Also attributing the value of physicality to her writing process, Gesa Kirsch thanks friends "for sharing training runs and martinis and for helping us find our new home" (Kirsch and Rohan xi). Joe Harris remarks in *Rewriting*, "I was also prodded along gently by my friend Pakis Bessias, who at the start of each of our Sunday morning runs would ask me how much I had written the week before, and then congratulate me on whatever my answer was" (136). And Michelle Payne identifies cycling as an important prelude to writing: "Most mornings before I began to write the first draft of this book, my Cannondale [a bike] took me all through York and Ogunquit, Maine, keeping me focused, centered, and aware of the coastal beauty I could so easily forget." As in the earlier examples, Payne's comment suggests that writing could subsume her, make her forget about beauty and all that's beyond writing. The good stuff—coastal beauty, laughter, love, etc.—competes with the reality of writing. Writing is simultaneously co-immersive in life activities and cut off from them. An opening up to and closing off from the world, writing occupies an ambivalent location for most writers, at least those who choose to comment on it. W. Ross Winterowd describes the inner/outer tension as follows, "Writing is the most human of actions; it forces you to live through your ideas and your experiences, and to realize that the two are not strictly separable" (341).

In addition to the way writing competes in these accounts with not-writing, the above examples are striking for another reason. They feature active, able bodies intermingled with good feeling and writing. In reviewing hundreds of acknowledgments, a handful of which appeared in books explicitly focused on disability issues, I uncovered none that addressed bodily impairment in relation to writing production. Only after receiving a recommendation from a reviewer of this manuscript did I find Michael Harker's acknowledgment in *The Lure of Literacy* in which he thanks a cystic fibrosis clinic. Harker writes, "Since receiving my diagnosis and learning how to manage complications that come from living with CF, I have developed a new appreciation for many things in my life. To be sure, I cherish each day that I breathe freely, especially those days when I find myself surrounded by friends and family" (viii).

Given the imperatives toward good feeling that guide acknowledgments, it's not surprising that able-bodied writing experiences dominate, that disabled bodies literally don't fit in this overly positive genre. What's missing in this context is the sort of reveal that Michelle Gibson makes in her short essay "Revising a (Writer's) Life: Writing with Disability." As multiple sclerosis advances, Gibson explains that she can no longer type: "[M]y hands have weakened and become uncoordinated, so I have had to revise the very basic ways I write and interact with my computer. I now spend my days wearing a headphone that controls my computer through voice recognition software" (13). The absence of disabled bodies in acknowledgments means that we end up with an image of writing as for the "fit," even as a form of "fitness" that does not reflect the realities of non-normative embodiments. While I recognize that acknowledgments are not the exclusive venue for challenging images of writing bodies, I also believe that the dominance of able bodies in acknowledgments is symptomatic of a field that likes to project happiness onto writing, a penchant that both causes writing scholars to miss important insights about writing practices and reproduces, unwittingly or not, writing as able-bodied. Jay Dolmage writes about ableism as an ideology that "makes able-bodiedness compulsory" (22). It does so, he argues, by rendering "disability as abject, invisible, disposable, less than human, while able-bodiedness is represented as at once ideal, normal, and the mean or default" (22). Reading about bodily fitness and writing in acknowledgments (and thinking about my own tendency to link writing and running) makes me reflect on the extent to which acknowledgments index a kind of writing ableism consistent with Dolmage's contention.

FEELING SCRIPTS

"The pleasure of writing and the pain of its absence tells something crucial about the motivation to write and the way it springs from our instinct to communicate. It is a feeling that is essential both for our ability as writers and for our potential to interact as human beings."

– Alice W. Flaherty, *The Midnight Disease*

Despite what I've found (and not found) in acknowledgments, writing of course reproduces and uncovers bad feelings. While I haven't uncovered a meaningful number of examples beyond Slick's, I have discovered that Tom Waldrep's 1985 collection *Writers on Writing* offers valuable insight into how critical writers describe their craft. Waldrep's two-volume collection includes essays by rhetoricians who respond to the question, "How do you write?" (vii). When asked directly, and presented in essay form rather than in acknowledgments—the genre expectations seem particularly relevant here—writers appear eager to reveal their bad feelings about writing and to bemoan their slapdash writing habits. Among the many interesting answers to Waldrep's question is Knoblauch's confession that "writing is never, for me, the pure joy some people insist it can be" (135). Knoblauch associates bad affect and writing with blue-collar work, admitting that he's grown "accustomed to the feeling that I'd rather be doing something else, just as the welder has" (135). By aligning the physical demands of writing with physical labor, Knoblauch also aligns alienated labor with writing. In an essay, Sue Lorch presents a visually arresting, embodied image of "doing something else" other than writing: "I inevitably view the prospect of writing a mental set more commonly reserved for root canals and amputations: If it must be done, it must be done, but for God's sake, let us put it off as long as possible" (165). Lorch associates writing with extreme forms of physical pain and, in the case of amputation, devastating loss. While hyperbolic, these associations provide a glimpse of writing pain that can plague those for whom writing is a profession or desire.

59

With less fanfare, George Hillocks, Jr. admits in his acknowledgments that his wife "has understood my need to indulge in occasional depression and to find some level of isolation to work on the manuscript," a statement made especially evocative by the running narrative of positivity that frames it (xv). Before Hillocks gets here, he spends two full pages expressing gratitude for the support he received from friends, colleagues, and students. The six-sentence paragraph in which depression is mentioned is followed by more than half a page of cheerful gratitude—most immediately, a paragraph on generous, helpful readers during the manuscript preparation process. Hillocks does not belabor his negative feelings; instead, he positions them approximately half way through his acknowledgments, tucked unassumingly into a fleeting paragraph overwhelmed by the predominant positivity around it.

Robert Boice, in *Professors as Writers*, offers an explicit view of writing pain through excerpts like the following, drawn from his interviews with professors who experience writing problems:

> "You probably won't like this. I hate to write. At least I do now. I'd rather clean the house. . . . I'd rather do almost anything else. I mean writing is a strain. I remember straining to figure out what to say. And then *how* to say it. It's much easier to talk about my ideas."

> "Even before I tried to begin I was already thinking about how exhausted I'd be. How tired I'd be after flailing away for a few hours. Do you know what I mean? And I was tired, even though I wrote for only about an hour."

> "I'd rather not hunk about it because whenever I do, I think about how difficult it is for me. Writing does not come easily for me, if it comes at all. When it comes, it happens slowly, painfully. I write about as fast as a snail. . . . And about as well."

> "I just thought about writing and I realized that I have yet to build a body of knowledge, a major contribution. I'm not ready. I certainly wasn't ready then. In the past, my efforts have often led down dark, blind dead ends. Perhaps it's nonsense to believe that I can contribute." (22–23)

These accounts will likely reveal unsurprising realities to any academic writer, whether in relation to one's own or colleagues' difficulties with writing. Yet acknowledgments often fail to register even a single hint of bad affect. Indeed, as already established, they are characterized by a near prohibition of bad feelings such that writers largely banish narratives of failure, discontent, and disappointment, which presumably would mark them as affect aliens.

Acknowledgments, instead, store feelings, especially good ones, related to writing. What does this drive to stockpile and enact good feeling tell us about writing? In some ways it suggests that writers, composing acknowledgments as the last step in preparing a manuscript for publication, are blinded by success or completion enough to develop a cheery retrospective attitude toward writing (the same logic sometimes used jokingly by those who decide to have a second child). Also, though, accumulating good feeling in acknowledgments implies that negative feelings undermine credibility and professionalism and effectively spoil happiness imperatives. The writing killjoy, kin to Ahmed's "feminist killjoy," might "expose the bad feelings that get hidden, displaced, or negated under public signs of joy" (*Promise* 65). Making bad feelings public is bad taste, an inappropriate indulgence, particularly in light of a finished, published work in an extremely competitive scholarly publishing market. Genre conventions for acknowledgments are so entrenched that exposing bad feelings simply falls too far outside the normative. These conventions also seem to dictate coherent narratives about writing rather than encourage multiple intersecting ones that might contradict or challenge one another. That is, acknowledgments are, in effect, happy endings that appear at the beginning of a book. Then again, I'm sure that writing is good feeling for writers, that writing is not suffering or hardship for some writers, and acknowledgments simply provide a space where those real experiences are prioritized.

Composition studies as a discipline is especially invested in writing as good feeling since writing and its production organize the field; bad feelings around writing rarely divert attention long enough to influence conversations about disciplinarity, first-year writing requirements, and writing's empowering capability (this is certainly true for my own research). For example, as mentioned earlier in this chapter, attention to writer's block remains anemic in composition studies, and, if publications and conference presentations are a reliable barometer, basic writing continues to occupy a marginal location in scholarship (and in the academy). More promising turns to writing and bad affect, for lack of a better phrase, have emerged in relation to transnational language use and composition (Canagarajah, Translingual; Horner, Lu, Matsuda; Horner, Lu, Royster, and Trimbur) and code-meshing (Young et al.). In these works, writing is not only a matter of skill and hard work but also a cultural tableau through which identity and language tensions surface. Alternative feeling scripts emerge as students from a variety of backgrounds bump up against the (arbitrary) conventions of Standard English. Such varieties are partly visible in acknowledgments, as examples throughout this book attest, but, on the whole, ideologies of goodness, happiness, and fitness associated with writing are far more prominent. Whether a consequence of genre conventions, dominant feeling scripts, writing ideologies, or something else, ac-knowledgments are probably too bright-sided, to borrow Ehreinrich's phrase, and, as a result, end up glossing over much of what hurts about writing.

IMPLICATIONS FOR TEACHING AND RESEARCH

This chapter indicates that studying acknowledgements can uncover a hidden af-fective curriculum. Acknowledgments as archives of good feeling, balm to ward against bad feeling, provide context for considering how teaching strategies can highlight the underlife of writing, bringing to the fore some non-procedural elements of writing that otherwise might not get a hearing but are important to sustain writing. To that end, students could collect their own examples of acknowledgments and individually and collectively code themes that emerge therein. In addition to being an engaging and slightly unconventional research project that could involve undergraduate students in collecting, organizing, and analyzing data, such an exercise could become the basis for identifying writing partnerships—particularly, in this case, with feelings. To what extent is writing aligned with feeling for students? What kinds of feelings? What associations are linked to those feelings? How do those associations bear on writing processes, habits, dispositions? Such openings might create permissive spaces for both ar-ticulating and valuing an affective continuum linked to writing. This, in turn, could prompt further research on writing difficulties—writer's block and popu-lation-specific writing issues (i.e., second language learners, veterans, trauma vic-tims)—an area of study that deserves fuller treatment than it currently receives.

Writing acknowledgments to accompany writing assignments, as Joe Harris advocates in *Rewriting*, also has benefits, even if only to generate awareness of the always collaborative relationships built into any scene of writing. Consider-ing the affective issues explored in this chapter, students might use the genre to chart the emotional work of writing, its highs, lows, and plateaus. This kind of mapping could be just as useful to faculty as to student writers themselves by motivating pedagogical methods that value embodied, affective experiences of writing. Writing is very often experienced as an endurance activity that takes a physical and emotional toll. That toll likely plays out in how students perceive writing and orient to it. What do we want students to feel? How does feeling re-late to writing? Why is it important to acknowledge bad feelings about writing? What kinds of bodies show up in acknowledgments and why?

The next chapter continues my exploration of writing partners in acknowl-edgments by turning to how writers narrate their experiences of inhabiting time. Attention to temporal materialities of writing brings focus to one of its most basic dimensions: how writing happens.

CHAPTER 3
ACKNOWLEDGING TIME

"No matter how much we may feel that our thought takes weightless flight, or that its velocity transcends time, mental processes work within biological materiality and have actual duration."

– Eva Hoffman, *Time*

"A much-longed-for faculty professional leave permitted me the privilege of research, contemplation, and time to write. There is no better gift than time."

– Jacqueline Jones Royster, *Feminist Rhetorical Practices* (with Kirsch)

While working on this book, I have occasionally recorded my screen to see what my writing looks like in real time. Most notable is that, in any fifteen-minute period, so little happens. A typical episode shows me copying and pasting text, typing five to six words, deleting two of them, and the cursor blinking at the last deletion point while minutes pass. These slow increments of text production, characterized by seemingly minor additions and deletions, likely make up the real-time act of writing for many of us. The resulting impression is that writing doesn't look like much. Screen capture, of course, is limited in what it can record because much of writing happens off-screen: looking out the window, readjusting a chair, petting a cat, drinking coffee, reading and rereading, thinking, listening to music. After reviewing several of these screen captures, I remain amazed that my writing has filled pages when it appears that I accomplish so very little at any given moment.

The underwhelming documentation of writing in situ reveals writing as optimistic and future-oriented—how else to explain why so many people do this slow-moving thing over and over again, presumably believing it will amount to something? As we read how a writer traces the lineage of a project in acknowledgments, we realize that she had to decide, at some earlier point, that the project was worth undertaking for a perhaps undetermined amount of time. She had to envision a future in which the work would be completed. Acknowledgments themselves might be the site through which to visualize a future, as writers very often imagine, during a writing project, how they will write the acknowledgments when the writing is finally done. In addition to being future-oriented, acknowledgments are tied up with memory: the writer looks back at how she completed the work and records what seems at the moment of completion to be major influences, supports, and so forth. The genre exerts a pressure to remember and to document. No doubt this real or imagined pressure, in addition to what might be called genre coercion, produces a need for narrative, a need arguably fulfilled by the genre of acknowledgments.

In many acknowledgments, writing seems to require a destabilized present. Writers lose track of time; writing exerts weightlessness even as reality thumps all around. Joseph Williams' preface to *Style* captures both writing's weightlessness and its rootedness in a demanding present: "And finally, to my family—my thanks for your love and support and understanding, especially when Daddy's 'just one minute' stretched to an hour or two" (n.p.). Contrast Williams' ability to disappear into his writing with Adrienne Rich's comment in *Of Woman Born* (not part of an acknowledgment) about the difficulty of writing as children make claims on her time:

> The child (or children) might be absorbed in busyness, in
> his own dreamworld; but as soon as he felt me gliding into
> a world which did not include him, he would come to pull
> at my hand, ask for help, punch at the typewriter keys. And
> I would feel his wants at such a moment as fraudulent, as
> an attempt moreover to defraud me of living even for fifteen
> minutes as myself. (23)

Time is an urgency in Rich's account precisely because she doesn't enjoy its availability. Here and elsewhere, the grammar of time is insistent, percussive, defined by moments of near transcendence interrupted by the heaviness of daily life, which, in Rich's account, includes the gendered demands of children. For Williams, another kind of gendered demand emerges, one characterized by the lightness of falling into writing and bracketing, at least for an hour or two, children's needs. For a contrastive view, Judith Goleman, in her acknowledgment, references Margaret Mead's response to Harriet Beecher Stowe, who complained that "she couldn't get any writing done because her baby cried so much" (xxii). Mead countered that she wasn't able to get writing done "because the baby smiled so much" (qtd. in Goleman xxii). Building on Mead's counter-intuitive retort, Goleman addresses the productive role of a child in her composing life when she writes that "the baby's smiles, if anything, made writing more possible, and this is an acknowledgment I want to make as I send this book out to future writers" (xxii). Time (and, as it turns out, smiles) is indeed a "gift," as Royster writes in her acknowledgment cited in the epigraph, one inflected by social arrangements of various kinds.

Despite Williams' seemingly unfettered disappearance for hours, even "weightless flight," as Eva Hoffman terms it, cannot elude time's thickness, its pressures and delights, its inescapable imprint. Weightlessness may be a feeling for some—a material reality, for others—but writing is irrefutably inseparable from time. In fact, writing's distinguishing feature might be that it unfolds in increments, revealing and becoming itself over time. That is, writing (the act) produces writing (the text) over time, and in so doing, writing (the act) becomes itself (the text). This idea is embodied in the commonplace yet arguably robust formulation of writing as a process. Process indicates creation over time even as it also denotes what Berthoff calls "allatonceness," the multidirectional demands particular to organizing language into written form.

The incremental aspect of writing is clearly visible as writers trace debts in acknowledgments. They frequently do so by emphasizing the long established origins that led to the final product. So, for instance, some identify "graduate school" as a starting point (Schell in Schell and Stock) or reveal the long timeline of a project—"this book is the result of seven years' work" (Hawhee, *Moving*)—or announce an unidentifiable single point of origin: "This book has deep roots" (Dunbar-Odom). These descriptions provide glimpses of how writing inhabits time, an emphasis that might more substantively affect writing theory and pedagogy than it does currently. Temporal materiality, more often than not, gets little attention, though this is changing as digital and multimodal pedagogies foreground the pace of composing when working with a wide range of tools, often in collaborative contexts.

Embodied realities of how we inhabit time while writing are remembered only vaguely once a project is complete, perhaps one reason why writing acknowledgments in fresh language that skirts genre conventions can be so challenging. Mikhail Bakhtin's concept of the chronotope, which describes how time and space are represented in literary texts, is useful here. For Bakhtin, the chronotope is an expression of genre-specific representations of time; for example, increments of time characteristic of an epic differ substantially from those of a lyric poem. Bakhtin explains, "In the literary artistic chronotope, spatial and temporal indicators are fused into one carefully thought-out, concrete whole. Time, as it were, thickens, takes on flesh, becomes artistically visible; likewise, space becomes charged and responsive to the movements of time, plot and history. This intersection of axes and fusion of indicators characterizes the artistic chronotope" (84).

Examining writers' constructions of time in acknowledgments offers one view of time "thickening," a wonderful phrase that aptly describes time's density, always inadequately represented in language. Writing time is thick with bodies, feelings, materials, others, and what John Tomlinson, in *The Culture of Speed*, calls "sedentary speed," or speed that is not connected to physical movement. That is, writing requires some element of stillness, which may of course be punctuated by activity to interrupt the sedentary pose of writing, and often is, judging by the accounts of running, walking, swimming, and bicycling described in acknowledgments. The simultaneously familiar and inscrutable qualities of the relationship between stillness and the forward orientation of writing complicates even the most basic commonplaces, like process and product—general terms that cannot help but gloss more nuanced experiences of writing.

Paul Prior and Jody Shipka make a similar point in "Chronotopic Lamination," in which they report on writers' literate activity as examined in four case studies. They begin with an example from one of their participants, a psychology professor who revises an article at home while doing laundry:

> She sets the buzzer on the dryer so that approximately every
> 45 minutes to an hour she is pulled away from the text to
> tend the laundry downstairs. As she empties the dryer, sorts
> and folds, reloads, her mind wanders a bit and she begins to
> recall things she wanted to do with the text, begins to think of
> new questions or ideas, things that she had not been recall-
> ing or thinking of as she focused on the text when she was
> upstairs minutes before. She perceives this break from the
> text, this opportunity to reflect, as a very productive part of
> the process. (180)

Time-based writing platforms perform a similar function vis-à-vis apps and online programs like the Pomodoro Technique, a writing timer that structures writing into 25 minute increments, punctuated by 5- or 15-minute breaks, during which users are encouraged to walk around, practice office yoga, or otherwise engage in some physical activity. A variation on Pomodoro that bills itself as more fluid, the Marinara timer (apparently Italian food provides a promising basis for timed writing) allows users—including teams of writers—to set whatever time increments they prefer. While writers could just as easily use their own timers to structure writing time, there seems to be something generative about a specialized writing timer, perhaps because it is sanctioned as a "method" or "technique."

A number of online writing tools embody the time-space fusion that Bakhtin attributes to the chronotope, as they prioritize daily word count (Word Counter), create a writing-focused window that disables access to the web and social media for a set period of time (SelfControl), and offer distraction-free spaces for writing. In that last category, for instance, is OmmWriter, advertised as "your own private writing room where you can close the door behind you to focus on your writing in peace. Everywhere you go, you have access to a beautiful distraction-free writing environment where your authentic voice is free to go where it is meant to go" ("Welcome"). In each case, customizable timers, writing spaces, and programs "mediate activity" by distributing work tasks in particular ways, effectively creating a writing ecosystem that aims for sustainability (cf. Prior and Shipka 180).

While time- and space-based approaches to writing emphasize that writing happens in and over time, these approaches are themselves transitory; used during the process of writing, they are ultimately overshadowed by the final product. In other words, with the presence of a final product comes the erasure of time as it was actually spent during the process. Calling attention to time-space, as the chronotope does, highlights writing's fleeting yet thick temporality. Using this concept as a guide rather than an explicit interpretive tool, this chapter focuses on how writers perceive and recount writing time, constructing narratives that make visible writing's temporality, usually well submerged, surfacing, if at all, in marginalia—dedications, acknowledgments, prefaces, and notes.

Acknowledgments offer a filtered, certainly incomplete, and partial view of that surfacing, but they nonetheless constitute a rich site of study because time emerges without prompting, in response to no particular expectation. When writers choose to narrate writing time experiences, what do they say? What constructs of cognition and writing emerge? What can we learn about writing, about teaching writing, through explicit attention to time? I'm particularly interested in understanding how writers identify time as an orienting device that gestures both to a writing past and to writing's future, a horizon of possibility. To think of writing as possibility is to view it as a series of promises that we make to ourselves and to readers; each incremental form of progress, no matter how ensconced in unease, gets us closer to a realized object. To return again and again to writing, without full knowledge of what those returns will bear, enacts possibility. Time, as a writing partner that intersects with possibility, attachment, and endurance, is made visible in acknowledgments, as I'll demonstrate in this chapter. Throughout, "time" represents an indexical concept that corresponds to writers' references to duration and indeterminate origins of a project, interruptions, wandering, shifting intellectual interests during the course of a career, losing oneself while writing, temporally based technologies, and cultural context as it intersects with writing. These references, which I excerpted from 25 acknowledgments, are organized into four sections that move from micro- to macro-scaled considerations of time. The first two sections, Elliptical Time and Slow Writing, focus on rhythm and pacing as writing partners identified in acknowledgments; the last two, Cultural Time and Composition Time, move outward to address how writing and time circulate in cultural and disciplinary composing contexts.

ELLIPTICAL TIME

Descriptions of writing as serendipitous wandering emerge in writers' representations of time in acknowledgments. Embedded in such descriptions are very often forms of physical and intellectual movement as well as distributed circuitry through which ideas circulate and then take form. For example, Carl Knappett, in *Thinking Through Material Culture*, identifies an "indispensable" resource for his project as "time to head off along blind alleys and find a way back again" (vi–viii). The wandering necessary to complete his project, an archaeological study that seeks to understand "the status of objects and of the humans producing and using them" (vii), is central to Knappett's thinking and writing. Perhaps commonplace, he calls our attention to writing realities that figure minimally, if at all, in contemporary theories and practices of writing. That writing takes time and is propelled by not knowing, dead ends, and wrong turns is arguably part of the deep structure of academic writing permitted in acknowledgments and other marginal texts but rarely foregrounded in writing pedagogy and theory.

Among other things, what finished writing obscures is not only the daunting amount of real time that goes into making scholarly work, but also the traces of a writer's changing interests that form over time. Such disclosures are commonplace in acknowledgments: "The roots of this book," writes Janice Lauer in *Invention in Rhetoric and Composition*, "go back decades. . . " (xvii). "This project represents the fulfillment of a dream deferred," begin Patricia Donahue and Gretchen Flesher Moon in their acknowledgment for *Local Histories*. They continue, "It was over fifteen years ago that the two of us, each year at the CCCC conference, began to share our concerns about the relative invisibility of certain kinds of institutions. . . " (xiii). N. Katherine Hayles describes her shifting orientation in the opening to *Writing Machines*: "This book is also an encoded record of a decade-long journey I have made as I moved from an orientation based in traditional literary criticism to one that took seriously my long-standing interests in technology from a literary point of view" (7).

Writers sometimes use acknowledgments to articulate detachment from a former self, the one who existed prior to or sometimes during the writing process. In her essay, "Rhythm and Pattern in a Composing Life," Louise Wetherbee Phelps vividly illustrates this detachment. Phelps describes what she calls a writing "slump," which for her is marked by "a sustained period of discouragement, depression, confusion, loss of confidence and competence" (25). The slump casts doubt on her abilities:

> I wrote in my daybook: "listless, lethargic, no ideas, no new
> ideas, all ideas seem worthless. Nothing connects or reminds
> or leads anywhere." (I knew, of course, that it would pass; but
> that was an intellectual conviction, not truly felt.) I marveled at
> the descriptions I had written earlier of the generative moment;
> later, when I had passed out of the slump I could not remember
> how it felt or how one could ever feel that way. (250)

Like Phelps, Brodkey, in her acknowledgments for *Writing Permitted in Designated Areas Only*, catalogs a disassociation that happens while writing:

> I probably owe my patience as a writer and teacher to the
> fact that while my prose falls apart far more often than it
> comes together, the pleasures of writing are unlike the other
> pleasures of my life. It's not that others are any more or less
> pleasurable, but that the unexpected moments in writing
> when time becomes space literally and figuratively move me.
> For the duration of the convergence of time and space, I am
> in my body and the body of my text. (ix)

Both writers juxtapose real-time writing with writing's ephemeral, immersive qualities. The passage of time while writing is, for Phelps, thick and slow-going while simultaneously a blip that becomes unimaginable in the aftermath of completed work. And Brodkey offers a mind-body fusion during which time and space do not impinge on writing's pleasures but function as a sort of weightless surround. For both, the grammar of time is a powerful way to narrate duration and periodicity of writing episodes.

Other writers similarly narrate gratitude in acknowledgments by referencing interactions that call to mind time-space configurations. Examples include the following:

> Several dear friends have encouraged or endured important
> parts of this project too, from instant messenger conversations
> to long phone calls to scraps scrawled on napkins in seedy
> establishments. (Banks xiv)

> To Sid Dobrin, Julie Drew, and Joe Hardin, who cheerfully
> endure the rambling and often intemperate e-mails in which
> I try to work through pesky theoretical problems and who,
> with equal cheer, let me know when I am writing nonsense.
> (Sánchez x)

> Also important were the many casual conversations with
> friends and colleagues over the years. When asked, 'So what's
> your book about?,' I had to articulate an answer, trying out
> various synopses in twenty-five words or less. My responses to
> these people met with instantaneous, enthusiastic validation,
> some leading to extended or multiple conversations. These
> conversations, individually and collectively, kept me keeping
> on. (Monroe x)

Online chatting, extended phone calls, dashed off napkin notes, "rambling" emails, spontaneous and extended conversations—all genres of exchange that have very specific temporal associations: fast, slow, intermittent, periodic, enduring, fleeting.

The grammar of time, particularly the dialectic between weightiness and weightlessness, might drive urges toward narrative cohesion in acknowledgments, where such cohesion might otherwise be lacking. For example, Mina Shaughnessy begins her preface to *Errors and Expectations* as follows: "I keep in my files a small folder of student papers that go back ten years in my teaching career" (vii). She notes that when she first read the "alien papers," she had no idea how to respond to or make sense of them. Looking at them a decade later, she writes in her preface, generates "no difficulty assessing the work to be done or believing that it can be done" (vii). "This book began that afternoon," writes Shaughnessy, "although I did not start to write it until some years later" (vii). Through this description, we glimpse the long history of a project, the way in which writing and time turn a problem and source of inquiry into an informed practice, and the certainty of an origin point, though, notably, not the origin point of physical writing itself. Even as Shaughnessy's description reads overly compact, for it seems unlikely that the most consuming work of her career can be traced back to one moment, her desire to construct a writing timeline, to give it an arc that moves from ignorance to enlightenment, strikes me as a narrative impulse illustrating more likely what is sayable about writing as a subject than what is actually descriptive of the process. That is, documenting writing often requires that we construct—maybe even concoct—time-based narratives, lending structure to an ephemeral process that, in practice, infrequently can be said to have discernible peaks and valleys.

It is probably more likely that writers experience chance moments and encounters over time that contribute to a project, even if unconsciously, after writing is underway. Robert Scholes, in his acknowledgment for *The Rise and Fall of English: Reconstructing English as a Discipline*, produces the most detailed such account that I've come across:

> As I have worked on this book over the past several years—
> and in particular, as I have tried to rethink, revise, and
> conclude it in the past few months—helpful books have often
> come to hand serendipitously. Some years ago the late Elmer
> Blistein gave me a copy of Walter Bronson's history of Brown
> University, which started me down the historical path I follow
> in Chapter 1. More recently while escorting Marcus and
> Sarah Smith through the wonders of Warren, Rhode Island,

where Brown began, the *Autobiography* of Billy Phelps literally fell into my hands from the shelves of an antique mall. Then, on a visit to Iowa City, I received much useful feedback from members of both the English and Education departments—and from John Gerber. . . . Even more recently my colleague Leonard Tennenhouse loaned me his copy of Franklin Court's book about the rise of English studies in British universities. To the authors of these books, as well as to the people who led me to them, I am grateful indeed—but there is no end to thanking the authors of books, so I will confine myself to mentioning those who have helped in others ways. (xiii)

The resources important to Scholes' project are attributed to people, books, strange occurrences (a book "literally fell into [his] hands"), accounted for in time increments—years, months—and narrativized through temporal markers like "started me down," "recently," "even more recently," and "then." His some-times improbable narrative mimics the subtitle of his book by reconstructing the path he took to tell this story of disciplinarity. What really comes through is that the act of writing is but one piece of the story; other pieces include writing's partnership with books, histories, chance, others, and time—ever-present recipients of gratitude.

SLOW WRITING

"It is nearly three years now since I first started developing the ideas for this anthology."
– Carmen Luke, *Feminisms and Pedagogies of Everyday Life*

"We especially thank Lil Brannon for her vision of a feminist project that would place differences among women at its center. That vision has helped sustain us from the spring of 1993, when this collection was begun, through the arduous process that brought it to completion [five years later]."
– Susan C. Jarratt and Lynn Worsham,
Feminism and Composition Studies

"The editors would like to acknowledge foremost the persistence and pa-tience of the contributors to this collection, who stayed with the project through its long initial planning stages and first publisher's bankruptcy."
– Christina Russell McDonald and Robert L. McDonald,
Teaching Writing: Landmarks and Horizons

Writing and publishing are forms of labor and labored processes. Writers develop ideas, persist through an "arduous process," withstand long "planning stages," and weather extraordinary circumstances, as did the McDonalds who endured a "publisher's bankruptcy" and deaths of contributors Robert J. Connors and Alan W. France prior to publication. This is to say, there are many reasons why writing slow is not only an effect of the difficulty of the task but also of the weightiness of reality bearing down on words and publications. Akin to the wandering advocated by Knappett and documented by Scholes, A. Suresh Canagarajah, in his acknowledgments for *A Geopolitics of Academic Writing*, depicts slowness as an opportunity for reflection and rejuvenation in the midst of a large project. Canagarajah writes, "My wife, Nanthini, daughters, Lavannya and Nivedhana, and son, Wiroshan (whose birth six months before the completion of this manuscript fortunately slowed down my writing and provided some invigorating time for reflection), continue to accommodate my life in scholarship and activism" (x). Writing cannot be bracketed from the moments and events that define us; it is part of the bundle, a commonplace observation, though one that has yet to influence seriously how writing is taught (the concluding chapter takes up this issue).

About the publication of *Writing Histories of Rhetoric* in 1994, Victor Vitanza reflects, "The particular book project—if I can assign it a place on the calendar—began in 1988" (xi). Even though instantaneous writing is everywhere around us thanks to social media, slow writing remains a reality for many writers, though a less visible one because it is less easily documented than, say, a tweet, Pinterest entry, or other mediated platform for quick writing. This might be why Doug Hesse, in "Writing and Time," argues that despite the ubiquity of writing in our culture, "relatively little of it happens in extended chunks drafted and revised over time. . . . We master the bon mot, we excel at snark" (1). Ultimately, he calls for "writing that takes time, both measured by episodes marked by butts in the chair but also episodes shaping over days and weeks. I'm not saying that such writing is nobler than the quick sprints of contemporary composition; it just provides a healthy counter-balance to frenetic fragmentation. Our writing ecologies need an increment of slow . . ." (5). Judging by writers' accounts in acknowledgments (as well as by my colleagues' and my own processes), I believe that slow writing is unthreatened and in fact, for critical work of any kind, normative (though it's less flashy and receives no attention in the mass media). What's perhaps less stable—and more consistent with Hesse's observation—are forms of documentation and systems of value that affirm slow writing as a practice that has worth. "Speed," writes John Tomlinson, "is always a matter of cultural value" (3). Since modernity, speed has been associated with "vigor and vitality" (4), forming a relatively coherent set of attitudes and values that adhere to speed. Thus Hesse's call for "writing ecologies" with "an increment of slow" arises as a counter-balance to the systemic embrace of speed and its virtues.

The slow speed of writing conjures associations with writer's block and general difficulty; in direct contrast with the vigor of speed, slow writing telegraphs weakness and stasis, and, in some cases, mental instability, as is evident in filmic representations of blocked writers in movies such as *Barton Fink* and *The Shining*. Yet slowness, patience, and generally being in the moment while writing have pleasures as well as convincing justifications. Slow writing may be attributable to stages of invention that do not defer to linear time. In "Rhythm and Pattern in a Composing Life," Louise Wetherbee Phelps describes her critical writing process:

> After a while I discovered that there is a natural rhythm to
> creativity that cannot be altered simply by will power. When
> I chart the ebb and flow of generativity in my composing life,
> there are broad, slowly changing tides representing my power
> to compose over a period of time, and little waves and swells
> day to day, minute to minute. I am particularly susceptible to
> the ebb of creative energy in transition periods between work
> activities that are differently paced. (250)

Writing, pace, and creativity shape how writing inhabits time and, conversely, how time inflects writing.

The dialectical relationship between writing and time is plainly evident in Lisa Ede's acknowledgments for *Situating Composition*. Spanning nine years, the final product reflects Ede's sense of responsibility as a researcher as well as genre and voice goals she set for herself. Charting her progress via the table of contents and its transformations, she writes, "The first table of contents for this study that I have in my files is dated August 14, 1994. By the time this book was completed in September 2003, this table of contents had gone through nineteen iterations" (xiv). Ede explains her process as follows:

> I often approach issues in composition studies analogically via
> research in such related areas as feminist theory, critical peda-
> gogy, and cultural studies, and I needed time to read and digest
> this research. I also needed time to develop the blurred genre
> approach that characterizes this study. . . . Moreover, while the
> style and approach of *Situating Composition* are hardly radical,
> I invested a good deal of effort and time in trying to write a
> text that—while most directly addressed to other scholars in

the field—might be accessible to others engaged in the work of composition, should they find their way to it. (xiv)

She adds that her mention of the "material conditions surrounding [her] work" pushes against the way "scholarly books and articles seem to appear magically out of nowhere. Such virgin births threaten to mystify the very material processes and collaborations that enable one scholar to bring a project to completion, while another finds it difficult to do so" (xiv-xv).

We can fruitfully attach Ede's temporal, materially conscious articulation of writing and its labors to Sara Ahmed's framing of writing time as embedded in social structures and arrangements. For Ahmed, time is always bound up with identity in some way. Referring to Adrienne Rich's observation about children and writing, Ahmed notes:

> This loss of time for writing feels like a loss of your own time, as you are returned to the work of giving your attention to the children. One does not need to posit any essential difference to note that there is a political economy of attention: there is an uneven distribution of attention time among those who arrive at the writing table, which affects what they can do once they arrive (and of course, many do not even make it). For some, having time for writing, which means time to face the table upon which writing happens, becomes an orientation that is not available given the ongoing labor of other attachments, which literally pull them away. ("Orientations" 250)

Taken together, Ede and Ahmed develop a theory of writing that foregrounds temporality, materiality, and attention practices. Writing surfaces as an incremental craft that is shaped by what adheres to us as political, social animals.

CULTURAL TIME

In other instances, acknowledgments anchor writing time in personal, intellectual, and/or cultural time. Ann Berthoff, writing with James Stephens in her 1988 edition of *Forming/Thinking/Writing*, originally published in 1978, writes with palpable disappointment about persistent stasis in educational practices in the U.S.: "I was thinking about this book during the days of campus protest against American action in Indochina, when I shared the hope of many that thoughtful, substantial changes in attitudes toward education could be institutionalized. They have not been, and one result is that illiteracy is by now a national crisis" (Preface, n.p.). I presume Berthoff is referring to *A Nation at Risk: The Imperative for Educational Reform*, commissioned by President Reagan and published by the National Commission on Excellence in Education in 1983. That incendiary report likens the alleged mediocrity of education (unsupported by research of any kind) to a declaration of war on our nation. The paranoia of this political moment—Americans are falling behind the rest of the world!—reflected the Cold War ethos and the jitters generated by a sputtering economy. That *A Nation at Risk* was a savvy political tool masked as an actual study of education in this country must have been chilling to progressive educators like Berthoff.

In another example of how the cultural time of the 1980s is expressed in acknowledgments, Ira Shor, in the second printing of *Critical Teaching and Everyday Life*, explains his reasons for not revising the manuscript. First published in 1980, with the second edition printed in 1987, the book represents for Shor a message in a bottle:

> I tell myself a few things about the passing of time: You can't escape your past, but neither will it desert you. Our experiences are cushions to fall back on when the going gets tough, as well as sources of energy that help us push ahead. They can also limit how far we can go and control what we choose to do. It's indispensable to know the past with a fearless intimacy and a critical detachment, but it's a great mistake to rewrite it. So, I don't want to revise this book. Not only does it continue to help teachers to transform their classroom practice, but it captures what I thought, felt, and did at a crucial moment in my life, in my teaching, and in a fateful episode of cultural democracy. (viii)

Writing is rooted in cultural and political time, and functions as a symptom of the state of democracy. Just as we cannot go back in time, release ourselves entirely from its grip, get too comfortable in the safety of the past, Shor suggests that we cannot discount the imprint of cultural time on intellectual work and its vitality in any given moment.

Emphasizing that imprint as the motivation to revise rather than preserve, Erika Lindemann begins her preface of the third edition of *A Rhetoric for Writing Teachers* by explaining why she felt compelled to revise the first edition of her book. For the 1995 edition, Lindemann reflects on the major changes in the field and in her own practices since the original 1980 publication:

> I am no longer the teacher I was when the first edition of *A Rhetoric for Writing Teachers* appeared. My students and my experiences in the classroom have changed me—and this book as well. In trying to make this an honest book, I have

> questioned and revised the suggestions it makes, the support
> for my claims, the examples, the order of chapters, occasional-
> ly even the tone of voice. In the process, I've had the privilege
> of wrestling with words written fifteen years ago—a construc-
> tive irritation if ever there were one—and of remembering the
> good company of students, teachers, and readers who contrib-
> uted to this project. (x)

The passage of time ages the book in ways Lindemann cannot abide; revision is a way of reckoning with a destabilized present, a way of looking forward rather than honoring what writing "captures," or holds in place as a record of cultural time, as in Shor's account. For both, though, explicit decisions emerge about how to acknowledge time and its significance to writing and the always growing gap between the record and the now.

Still others address cultural time not so much by explicitly calling attention to the passage of time but by performing something of the contemporary mo-ment through the act of writing. Take, for example, this excerpt from Adam Banks' 2006 acknowledgment in *Race, Rhetoric, and Technology*:

> My chair and mentor, Keith Gilyard—if Bill Russell the
> player/coach had Erving's flavor, Oscar's ability to take over,
> the Iceman's finger roll, and Darryl Dawkins' backboard
> breaking thunder, he might have been close to what you bring
> the academy. You let a playa handle the rock and you always
> coached the game, gave me the support to get through and
> the challenge to get over. You made that barbershop your
> office became, that woodshed, real, putting more Black minds
> out in the academy in a shorter time than anybody I've ever
> seen. You meant everything to my getting out here and give
> a hell of an example of what intellectual work can be. I can't
> thank you enough for letting me get on the roster. (xiii–xiv)

Banks moves fluidly between home and school languages, just as he does between academic and basketball references, while honoring his mentor whose effects are both personal and political. Gilyard put Banks "on the roster," as he did many others, "putting more Black minds out in the academy in a shorter time than anybody I've ever seen." In this short passage (and in the complete ac-knowledgment), Banks communicates the urgency of nurturing Black students. He also constructs a community through language use and cultural references, configuring acknowledgments as a space that can (and should) account for the time of writing, a time during which the mentoring of black students in composition studies—and in the academy, more broadly—is still novel enough to be called out in explicit ways.

COMPOSITION TIME

Time has preoccupied the field of composition studies from its beginnings, though this is not obvious when surveying existing scholarship. That is, with the exception of early process research. Emig, for example, in her 1971 landmark study, *The Composing Processes of Twelfth Graders*, develops an outline of her study participants' writing processes in which she includes the time-sensitive "tempo of composing" and its subcategory, "combinations of composing and hesitational behaviors" (35). Under "other observed behaviors," Emig lists "silence" and "vocalized hesitation phenomena" (35). Major categories in the outline include "starting" and "stopping," both of which link to subcategories for "contexts and conditions under which writing" started and stopped, and "interveners and interventions" (34–35). Emig again addressed temporality and writing, though this time in partnership with technology and memory, in "Hand, Eye, Brain," originally published in 1978. In her discussion of the value of writing by hand, Emig notes that doing so "keeps the process slowed down," which can yield surprises, though she also mentions as potential disadvantages that "a slow pace" can cause writers to "lose as well as find material since such a pace obviously puts a greater strain on the memory" (112). During the same period, Elbow, in *Writing Without Teachers*, advocates the process approach for which he has become nearly synonymous, contending that "[m]ost processes engaged in by live organisms are cyclic, developmental processes that run through time and end up different from how they began" (33). Because scholars were actively building a case for resisting static approaches to writing pedagogy that prioritized a product, it makes sense that early research names time explicitly as a significant writing partner.

In the aftermath of process writing's high water mark, though, time is typically not foregrounded but is a subject of interest in conjunction with something else. It's worth noting, however, that the very origins of the field are inextricably bound up with time in the form of timed writing exams, most famously the exam instituted by Harvard in 1874 that led to the development of the nation's first college-level required writing course. Timed writing exams for placement have long been staples in composition programs, despite ongoing debates about their validity (see Perelman; White). Time also looms over strategies for managing the paper "load," a subject that has gotten considerable attention on a cyclical basis (see, e.g., Golub; Jago). Time is a precious research resource, particularly in relation to longitudinal studies that span a year or more in an effort to understand how writing skills change and evolve. And, of course, time regulates academic culture, where careers are structured by "clocks" and we speak of "writing time" and "teaching time."

In looking back at the emergence of composition courses in the United States, it's impossible to detach them from the low-status labor force they demanded and reproduced. The extreme time commitment required of the first composition teachers is documented to persuasive effect by Robert Connors, among others. For example, Connors cites the Hopkins Report, produced in 1913, which was based on surveys completed during a four-year period between 1909 and 1913 by American composition teachers. Connors quotes the following findings from the report:

> The average necessary duty of an English instructor according
> to the class and hour standards in effect was almost double
> (approximately 175 percent) that of an instructor in any of
> the other departments concerned. . . . The theme reading
> labor expected of a college freshman composition instructor is
> more than double (250 percent) that which can be carried on
> without undue physical strain. . . . Conscientious and efficient
> teachers are brought to actual physical collapse and driven from
> the profession. . . . (qtd. in Connors, "Rhetoric" 71)

We cannot outrun the time inequity woven into the origins of composition courses. It's no surprise that time frequently emerges in relation to contingent workers in the field who teach four or five sections a term, often at different institutions, in stressful, poorly compensated conditions.

Teaching is limited by time in ways that drive pedagogical theory and practice, for what we can do in a given time frame necessarily shapes pedagogy. The minimal explicit references to time in writing pedagogy are in some ways reasonable given that time is a fundamental, rather than exceptional or extraordinary, component of experience and reality. Time is woven into familiar terms and practices without much fanfare. Freewriting, quick writing, chat room discussions, twitter use, and "speed-dating" peer review sessions are explicitly time-bound activities. Revision is often described as a recursive process involving, as Nancy Sommers pointed out in 1980, "significant recurring activities—with different levels of attention and different agendas for each cycle" (386). Those different levels and agendas remind me of the oft-heard admonition to treat revision as a process of "re-seeing," for which time passage and cyclical returns are integral to encountering a piece of writing with fresh eyes. This makes sense if, with Hoffman, we agree that the "problem of time is inseparable from that of meaning" (185), as meaning emerges (or gets obscured) in and over time, often as a result of a series of returns.

In his 1991 "Reflections on Academic Discourse," Peter Elbow calls for teaching both "nonacademic" and "academic" discourse in first-year writing classrooms. One foundation for his argument has to do with time. "[L]ife is long and college is short," writes Elbow, as he begins to build his case for teaching writing as a life-long pursuit rather than an exercise mired in the conventions of academic discourse (if there really is such a thing). For him, "the best test of a writing course is whether it makes students more likely to use writing in their lives" (136). This rationale is very similar to what I heard from a running coach who was training a group of novice joggers to prepare for a marathon. He was fond of saying that whether or not we ever ran another marathon was completely irrelevant to him; he wanted us to become life-long runners—that would really mean something. Discussions of writing transfer, likewise, are geared toward writing futurity, or how students will be able to apply the skills and strategies they develop in one course to unforeseen sites of writing activity.

Elizabeth Wardle and Douglas Downs, in their first articulation of the writing about writing pedagogy, frame their expectations around time constraints, noting that imperfect student writing is a reasonable outcome. Because their students are conducting field research, often for the first time, they have a lot to learn. They write that "accepting imperfect work recognizes important truths about all research writing: it takes a long time, is inevitably imperfect, and requires extensive revision. The rewards of accepting imperfection as part of a challenging research and writing curriculum outweigh the deficiencies of courses in which students produce more-polished but less-demanding and realistic writing assignments" (575). This claim is consistent with literature on transfer, which argues that writing improvement is difficult to track because it is progressive rather than evident during a 10- or 15-week course, for example. In the second edition of *Helping Students Write Well*, Barbara Walvoord articulates a familiar refrain among writing specialists, particularly WPAs who field questions from colleagues across the disciplines about student writing: "Writing is so complex an activity, so closely tied to a person's intellectual development, that it must be nurtured and practiced over all the years of a student's schooling and in every curricular area" (4).

Constructs of time and orienting oneself in relation to then, now, and later are of particular significance to democratizing pedagogies geared toward change. To take perhaps the most famous example, Paulo Freire frames problem-posing education in temporal terms when he calls it "revolutionary futurity" (72). Such education, he writes, "corresponds to the historical nature of man. Hence, it affirms men as beings who transcend themselves, who move forward and look ahead, for whom immobility represents a fatal threat, for whom looking at the past must only be a means of understanding more clearly what and who they are so that they can more wisely build the future" (72). Also geared toward change, though through less revolutionary methods, contemplative pedagogies make conscious use of time to stimulate good thinking in the service of rhetorical action, particularly argumentation. For example, Barry Kroll, in *The Open Hand*, describes how he teaches "meditation and mindfulness as practical arts that enhanc[e] ones' effectiveness in the world, especially in difficult conversations, interpersonal disputes, and arguments about divisive issues" (13). Likewise, in "Beyond Belief," Donna Strickland describes a pedagogical activity, inspired by Peter Elbow's believing game, called the "trying game." She includes two example reading prompts from her class, both of which make explicit use of time by asking students to pause, relax, and notice their bodies while reading (85). Both Kroll and Strickland advocate strategies of slowing down aimed at helping students learn how to pay attention to internal and external factors while communicating and reading.

PEDAGOGICAL TIMES

"If you think something is boring, try doing it for two minutes. If you still think it's boring, try it for four. If you still think it's boring, try it for eight, then sixteen, then thirty-two, and so on and so forth. Soon enough you'll find that it's really not boring at all."

– John Cage (see Asia)

In cartoonist and writer Lynda Barry's extraordinary pedagogical book *Syllabus*, she presents a compilation of activities, teaching notes, and syllabi for several drawing courses she teaches at the University of Wisconsin. Many of Barry's activities intentionally manipulate time to produce certain results and affects around creative work. Some rely on speed, producing work quickly without over-thinking and with the goal of building skills, habits, and confidence. For example, one activity requires students to spend three minutes drawing a house on fire that fills an entire page of a composition notebook (102). Other activities reinforce the value of simplicity and repetition, as illustrated by her approach to taking attendance. Students spend two minutes each class drawing self-portraits on index cards; she collects these in lieu of taking attendance and then returns the whole batch to students at the end of the course. "There are usually about 30 drawings in all, most of them completely forgotten until our last day of class," writes Barry. "My hope is that they see the extraordinary result of doing something as ordinary as drawing a 2-minute self-portrait on an index card twice a week" (57). Out of the mundane comes the extraordinary, an idea that might just as well inform Cage's advocacy of repetition.

In another effort to highlight ritual and repetition, Barry assigns a daily diary in which students color, write stories, and make drawings. In her note to the students about this assignment, she says,

> Daily practice with images both written and drawn is rare once we have lost our baby teeth and begin to think of ourselves as good at somethings and bad at other things. It's not that this isn't true . . . but the side effects are profound once we abandon a certain activity like drawing because we are bad at it. A certain state of mind (what McGilchrist might call 'attention') is also lost. A certain capacity of the mind is shuttered and for most people, it stays that way for life. (115)

Barry's explanation calls to mind similar claims made about writing journals, including the belief that ongoing, low-stakes writing helps to cultivate good habits and to practice paying attention to texts and to the world as a means for building writerly flexibility and confidence. In composition scholarship, journals have been variously extolled as a tool for settling students at the beginning of class, a site for recording informal thoughts about reading material, a free space for getting in the habit of writing with no concern for content, and a learning log for documenting development over time. The value (and utility) of journals has been linked, in one way or another, to efforts that capture a moment in time and that often require time commitments beyond the classroom. Barry's methods, too, prize independent, focused work not bracketed by classroom time that cultivates everyday life practices (not unlike Berthoff and Elbow's recommendations in relation to writing).

Because Barry models a pedagogical method that can be adapted to different learning tasks and environments, *Syllabus* is valuable to anyone who makes art, including writers, and to teachers of any subject. Barry's deliberate foregrounding of time as a partner of art-making is a powerful heuristic for writing instruction, particularly in terms of how teachers might more explicitly exploit the affordances of time for multiple purposes. If quick and repetitive—like freewriting can be, for example—time-conscious activities can increase muscle memory, reinforce the "ordinariness" of writing, and thereby build confidence; if slow and recursive, activities might coach deep attention, or what it means to stay with an idea over a sustained period and allow thinking to evolve.

Before outlining pedagogical approaches that exploit time as a resource for writing, I want to point out that the partnering of time and writing has been addressed in especially powerful ways by advocates of equitable pedagogies. For example, disability studies advocates suggest that teachers meet with students off campus when they can't make office hours, and disability policies common at most universities call attention to time as one resource that students with learning disabilities may need more flexibility with, whether in relation to turning in work, reading assigned materials, or participating synchronously or asynchronously in classroom discussion and/or group projects. In these cases and others, time is a resource directly relevant to learning and performing knowledge; it is a partner whose normative status cannot be assumed for all learners (see, e.g., Dunn; Lewiecki-Wilson and Brueggemann; Wilson and Lewiecki-Wilson). Pedagogical approaches that benefit students with disabilities may very well benefit all learners, as suggested by the authors cited above, a key insight of universal design principles in general.

Likewise, the unique circumstances of military veterans in college classrooms call for pedagogies that treat time as a special resource. In both disability and veteran-focused pedagogies, we are reminded of how social and personal temporalities encompass diversity, a reality that can sometimes become obscured by the linearity of institutional time. In a 2015 NCTE position statement, "Student Veterans in the College Composition Classroom: Realizing Their Strengths and Assessing Their Needs," organizers cite the Wounded Warrior Project's description of on-campus challenges for student veterans: "Participants cited such difficulties as being unable to move quickly from one class to the next across campus, hyper-alertness and anxiety caused by PTSD, difficulty concentrating due to TBI, and difficulty relating to other students" ("Student Veterans"). In terms of assignments, the statement notes that "[W]riting programs should have plans in place to accommodate veterans with Post-Traumatic Stress Disorder (PTSD) concerns and with Traumatic Brain Injury (TBI concerns), as both of these sometimes manifest in a need for additional time for reading and writing as well as difficulties concentrating and short-term memory loss" ("Student Veterans"). These excerpts reference diverse enactments of time in relation to learning: movement across campus; heightened sensitivity to environment, which surely is related to time and associated exigencies; organization of classroom time; the labor of reading and writing; and attention practices and memory capabilities. This position statement increases awareness of non-normative time, an awareness that can revise existing pedagogical approaches when we take seriously time as a partner whose affordances are much more than background to writing.

In that spirit, the remainder of this section generates some ideas aimed at using time in deliberate ways that call attention to it not so much as the condition of existence for teaching but as an explicit partner whose capabilities we can exploit for pedagogical purposes.

Scale back: Writing classes, especially required first-year courses, tend to include a series of scaffolded assignments that build on one another, adding complexity as they progress. It's not unusual for a FYC curriculum to include three or four major assignments (i.e., literacy narrative, rhetorical analysis, synthesis paper, and research project). While I have advocated for a curriculum at my institution that looks very much like the composite one suggested here, I have also come to question the value of completing four major assignments in one 10 or 14 week course. The pacing of such assignments is often rushed, particularly if factoring in time for reading, discussion, and multiple drafting, and can feel like a hustle. Before we settle into the conventions and requirements of one assignment and identify its problems or student confusion related to it, we begin prepping for the next one. The pace is often frenetic and does not allow for sitting with an idea as it changes and evolves through deliberative thinking, researching, and writing. Thus, it's worth experimenting with curricula in a way that allows writing to stretch and sprawl, the way it often does for scholarly writers, in unexpected ways.

Develop time-sensitive activities: In an effort to make time visible as a major ingredient of writing, we might ask students to conduct observations of peers, followed by interviews, to document what writing looks like in real time. In addition, students might record their screens during a writing session, share what they observe with classmates, and narrate to the class what they learn about writing by viewing their own screencasts as well as those of their peers. How exactly does writing unfold over time? What kinds of decision-making can we see on screen that tells us something about writing practices, problems, tendencies, and so forth? Such an approach might be especially useful in courses that adopt writing about writing pedagogies. Documentation of writing as it happens could form the basis of a research project.

Write together: Perhaps building on the "flipped" classroom model, use class time to write together (teacher too). In a recent graduate class, Critical Writing in English Studies, essentially a workshop for critical writers, I set aside one three-hour class period for writing together. Nearly every student in the class made a note of this session in the course evaluation, suggesting that I integrate more writing time into the class schedule during future iterations. I was not surprised to read this suggestion, as the session was charged with excitement; being in a room together with other writers created a positive vibe that allowed us all to be task-oriented. We also generated a valuable discussion at the end of the session about our goals for the three hours, our achievements, and what our next steps will be. Writing as an act in time became highly visible and material, a change from our usual post hoc conversations of writing as already made.

Enact different temporalities: My research has challenged me to consider how I might make room for non-normative temporalities in a classroom setting. Is it possible, in other words, to create the conditions necessary for students to wander down blind alleys; experience serendipity; feel lost; appreciate the hypnotic power of time disorientation while writing? I'm not sure, but I have experimented by relocating several class sessions to the stacks in our library, where I ask students to spend a class period browsing one section of the stacks, opening books and documenting provocative, troubling, or confusing sentences, references, and ideas that they come across. Students find a source in the bibliography of one book that sounds promising and then track down that book in the library (or on the internet). While this exercise was not a universal success by any means, some students reported that they fell into a sinkhole during these class sessions, forgetting that we were "in class" and enjoying the time to rummage, as it were, without clear direction or purpose. Because a great deal of critical writing seems to emerge from surprising connections and networks of ideas that could not be mapped beforehand, I like the idea of manufacturing a random reading day for the habits of mind it teaches (or unteaches) as well as the thinking and writing it could inspire. In these sessions, I foreground not content but time, a shift in focus that calls attention to research as bounded and concrete. That is, the experience helps us come to terms with research activity in real time, making it more tangible and something we can recount when we reconvene.

One thing is clear: time might be writing's most faithful partner, ambitious compass, fearsome threat. Acknowledgments offer a view of the micro- and macro-constructs of time that bear on writing and that constitute an always present partner. Writing is unthinkable outside of time structures, in other words, even if such structures are routinely under-emphasized in writing pedagogy. To view writing as that which we endure, withstand, and return to is to understand it as always inhabiting time and always pitched toward futurity. The next chapter extends the ongoing study of writing partners that show up in acknowledgments by focusing on other living creatures that take up residence in writers' space, time, and hearts. Drawing attention to animals in scenes of composing, chapter four sketches a broad theory of "withness" that considers how time and feeling as well as animals co-contribute to writing activities and experiences.

CHAPTER 4

ACKNOWLEDGING ANIMAL COMPANIONS

"[Writing] is least often an isolated, solitary act created *ex nihilo*, and most often a communal, consensual act, one that is essentially and naturally collaborative."

— Andrea Lunsford and Lisa Ede, "Why Write . . . Together"

and now sometimes I'm interviewed, they want to hear about
life and literature and I get drunk and hold up my cross-eyed,
shot, runover de-tailed cat and I say, "look, look
at *this*!"

but they don't understand, they say something like, "you
say you've been influenced by Celine?"

"no," I hold the cat up, "by what happens, by
things like this, by this, by *this*!"

— Charles Bukowski, "the history of a tough motherfucker"

In the acknowledgments section of my dissertation, I thanked various people—my mentor, committee members, family, friends—and then I wrote, "I also want to express my deep appreciation for Peanut and Tiny, who taught me the importance of wit, sound sleep, and playfulness. Peanut's acrobatics have especially convinced me of the importance of mobility and spunk" (*Cultural* vii). Eight years later in the acknowledgments of a book, I thanked "[t]hose feline wonders for daily consistency mixed with good doses of surprise and silliness" (*Doing* xvi).

I have come across mentions of animals by other writers in their acknowledgments, though these admittedly amount to a very small number overall, totaling less than ten mentions out of the hundreds of books I reviewed for this study. Unlike mentions of feeling or time, both of which emerged routinely in my research, animal gratitude was marginal within a marginal genre. Despite their scarcity, though, the minimal mentions of animals echoed the seemingly "natural" relationship between (creative and "great") writers and animals routinely represented in pop culture. The dominant tendency to make iconic the relationship between famous writers and animal companions led me to the fringes of written acknowledgments in books by a different class of writers: on the whole, those who are not famous, not identified as creative writers who, through imaginative craft, seem predisposed to have close relations with animal partners because they presumably work alone, surrounded by books and writing tools, and need a living creature to populate, not disturb, the abiding solitude.

In other words, following the bread trail I uncovered in a handful of acknowledgments by academic writers, I sought to learn more about how this group of writers would acknowledge animal companions as partners when asked directly. Thus, in addition to analyzing written acknowledgments, this chapter more broadly engages acknowledgments as a rhetoric of partner inclusion, the focus of my qualitative study.

COMPANION GRATITUDE

A friend of mine told me that before diving back into revisions of a long-abandoned writing project, she decided to adopt two cats. She didn't want to feel so alone while at home writing. If she could get away with it, she said, she would bring the cats to work with her. When I asked if she has friends at work to whom she can talk about her writing, she replied, "Yes, I do, but I don't want to talk about my work with anyone. I just want to *do* it with others around me."

As it turns out, this desire is not idiosyncratic. In 2013, *Times Higher Education* ran an opinion piece by philosophy professor Erin McKenna focused on pets in academic workplaces. Her institution, Pacific Lutheran University, has a permissive pet policy. She brings her Australian shepherds to the office with her because she is "more productive when Maeve, Tao and Kira are flopped around [her] desk." She cites studies focused on universities with "pet-friendly halls of residence," in which students have been found more likely to "persist to graduation." McKenna's linking of productivity and pets is reinforced by recent research showing that looking at animals stimulates oxytocin production, generating, in short, good feelings. And good feelings are linked to persistence, or continuing with a project for the long-term and weathering difficulty. In 2012 researchers at Hiroshima University conducted a study in which they "showed university students pictures of baby animals before completing various tasks" (Kliff). Another group of participants completed comparable tasks without viewing these images. The results showed that productivity was far and away highest among those who had seen the images (for similar research studies, see McQuerrey; Serpell).

This research, focused on intellectual tasks of various kinds, complements well-documented relationships, particularly on social media, between writers and animals. Animals and writing productivity (and/or avoidance) are often aligned, as illustrated in Figures 4.1 and 4.2, images posted by friends on my Facebook feed.

Figure 4.1: Writing with Salsa. Photo credit: Janice Fernheimer

Figure 4.2: Writing with Waylon. Photo credit: Allison Carr

In another post, a woman is reading in bed, flanked by a dog who is identified as her "research collaborator" (see Figure 4.3).

Figure 4.3: Cricket (human) reading with Abby (dog). Photo credit: Amy Lind

In this next photo, a graduate student works at her laptop with her friend's cat, named har, sitting just behind the computer (see Figure 4.4).

Figure 4.4: Writing with har. Photo credit: Chelsie Bryant

The thread with har reads as follows:

> First commenter: har's going to write my modernism paper
> for me.
>
> Second commenter: har writes everyone's papers. That's how
> I've gotten this far without dying.
>
> Third commenter: Can I borrow him this weekend? And can
> he write two at a time?
>
> Second commenter: Basically, har has superpowers. The fatter
> he gets, the more papers he can write.

Playful, distracted, wishful—most definitely. But the idea that har writes papers is also an expression of how people think through and with animals. Dwelling with companion animals generates a powerful relationality in everyday life and, as this chapter demonstrates, in writing lives as well. Writing is an engagement with ideas and language, of course, but also with the many others who make up our worlds.

This partnership is uniquely reflected in written acknowledgments and in acts of acknowledgment more generally, which recognizes and names the contributions of others to one's own existence, achievement, and/or situation. Both the genre of acknowledgments and the rhetorical act of acknowledging broadly construed get considerable attention in this chapter. This dual focus allows me to enhance my textual findings with the inclusion of voices and images of writers who, through their participation in my qualitative study, provide extratextual access to the world of "we" referenced in the introduction to this book. What does that world look like? When asked to expand on the human-animal partnership that written acknowledgments called to my attention, what do writers say?

As is probably apparent, the wider cultural context also informs my work in this chapter. Well-documented creative partnerships between animals and artists—writers, musicians, visual artists, and others—abound. Several years ago singer-songwriter Fiona Apple wrote an open letter to her fans in South America, explaining that she was canceling her tour to be with her dying dog Janet. Listing the ways in which Janet has been faithful to her and important to her well being, Apple notes that Janet was "under the piano when I wrote songs, barked any time I tried to record anything, and she was in the studio with me, all the time we recorded the last album" (Popova). The album is in some ways a product of their entwined relationship, which makes Janet's passing especially difficult for Apple; it's clear from her announcement that her creative work is not accomplished alone, but happens with her dog by her side, who participates by barking during recording sessions.

When it comes to writing, cats often seem to get top billing, perhaps due to what catophile Ernest Hemingway calls their "absolute emotional honesty." He continues, "human beings, for one reason or another, may hide their feelings, but a cat does not" (Minkel). Want tough critics or models of raw feeling, he seems to suggest, write with cats in your midst, an idea echoed in Figure 4,5, an image of the Floating Judgment Box.

Figure 4.5: Floating Judgment Box. Photo source: http://www.funnyjunk.com /Floating+judgment+box/funny-pictures/5367004/

The special alignment between cats and writers is ubiquitous. Perhaps the fact that writing requires a good deal of stillness has something to do with that connection—sitting before a desk, computer, or tablet for long stretches of time amounts to a lifestyle amenable to creatures who like to stretch out and recline in one spot, ideally while being stroked periodically. Cats do not need to be walked or let outside to relieve themselves. They are champion loungers, a point that comes up in my research when writers describe how cats help them persevere in a writing task by physically pressing on them, ultimately coaxing writers to stay put. In contrast, the breaks that dogs and other animals introduce into domestic scenes are perceived as assisting writers in a very different way—by instituting forced breaks that help writers gather their thoughts and return to writing feeling rejuvenated after a quick walk.

Returning to cats for a moment, "Writers and Kitties," a tumblr site with the tagline "Where literature has whiskers and pointy ears" includes photos of well-known literary and philosophical figures posed in various states of proximity with cats. We see, for example, Jean Paul Sartre proofreading with "Kitty" on his arm (see Figure 4.6); a dimly lit photo of Michel Foucault cuddling with a black kitty in the foreground, packed bookshelf in the background; and Yukio Mishima (pen name of author Kimitake Hiraoka) taking a drag from a cigarette while sitting at his cluttered desk and seemingly staring at a kitty who is watchfully positioned just in front of the desk. From behind, the cat appears to be intensely staring back (see Figure 4.7).

Figure 4.6: Sartre and Kitty. Photo source: http://writersandkitties.tumblr.com/

Representing a more pet-centric perspective, the Pets on Academia tumblr features mostly cats (some dogs) resting on or sitting next to academic materials in scenes largely absent of humans (see Figure 4.8). A typical image is accompanied by a caption that projects rhetorical agency onto the pet, constructing a sort of double for the writer, reader, and/or teacher who took the photo. That is, pets are ventriloquized, giving voice to the deep ambivalence that surrounds much academic work. Does this work matter? Is it anything? The captions express doubt, question the lifestyle required to complete academic work, and generally repeat the same gag over and over: "Your 'important' work? Meh." We see a paradigmatic example in figure 4.8.

And, so, all of the hard work and energy that went into your dissertation? In Achilles' world, you've created an excellent throne—little else. No doubt the self-effacing humor keeps high-minded views of academic work in check, making room for sentiment that I'd guess is fairly common among academics, sentiment that questions the significance of our work in the broader scheme of things. Images on Pets on Academia do not usually document attachment between human and animal (like Writers and Kitties) as much as they document the need for a nonhuman stand-in to help cope with (some aspects of) academic work (dense, time-consuming reading, endless grading, difficult writing) and lifestyle (late hours, blurred lines between work and life, excessive screen time). Many of the images telegraph wishful detachment from academia, the kind of aloofness that cats exude so effortlessly. Academic work does not respect a life-work balance but instead spreads and sprawls across desks, relationships, and time (again, much like cats).

Figure 4.7: Mishima and cat. Photo source: http://writersandkitties.tumblr.com/

Figure 4.8: "Achilles thinks my dissertation draft makes an excellent kitty dais."
Photo source: http://petsonacademia.tumblr.com/

By positioning pets as projections of their own doubts about academia, participants engage in imaginative flight as the other. Jonathan Safran Foer writes in the foreword to *Animals and the Human Imagination* that "our self-conception has always depended on how we imagine animal others" (x). The dialogue about har above illustrates this dialectic between self-conception and imagining animals. har functions as alter-ego of the writers, who project superpowers onto him and, by extension, onto themselves. The displacement of writing powers onto har is a way for the writers to humorously deflect their own feelings of powerlessness by locating those feelings in the enigmatic figure of a cat who patiently keeps them company as they write under deadline. The implication is that one can only accomplish the many writing tasks of graduate school through deployment of super-human powers.

This is not to say that animals are understood exclusively as stand-ins for human anxiety in the context of writing. As noted by participants in my research study detailed below, companion animals are most certainly not objects but subjects who contribute in significant ways to writerly identity and persistence. Attributing pets with agency reminds me of Potter's critique of bloated acknowledgments, discussed in the introduction, in which she remarks that pets should not be included in acknowledgments because, as she puts it, they "just do pet things." Much contemporary research in and around animal studies offers considerably more thoughtful approaches to understanding just what pets do for and with humans. Part of my aim in this chapter is to make visible what some of those understandings look like when applied to writing activities.

Much of my analysis addresses the idea of "withness," or the ways in which animals and humans, tangled together in everyday encounters, co-create writing experiences and spaces in large and small ways. Writing is defined, ultimately, by its radical withness, even as it can feel isolating and lonely—oppositions that emerge throughout my research. If writing is not exclusively a relay between mind and body, or mind and tool, then how do we describe it? And how would more chaotic descriptions of writing translate into theory and practice? Would they need to? Is writing ever dependent on the proximity of furry critters? On warm bodies pressing down, growling, or otherwise expressing affection, comfort, and closeness? One example of the sort of withness I have in mind appears in an exhibit called "In the Company of Animals," organized by The Morgan Library and Museum in New York, in cooperation with the literary journal *Ploughshares*, for which artists in their workspaces reflect on connections between animals and their creative work. Writer Emma Straub, in an online video, describes her cats as important to her writing process in numerous physical ways ("In the Company"). For instance, when her cat Killer is lying on her, she is less likely to stop writing and do something else. She will continue at her computer, even if she's hungry or has to go to the bathroom, essentially waiting out the cat and prolonging her writing time. Writing is deeply intertwined with Straub's context—sitting in bed with a laptop, weighed down by a resting cat—and with bodies as they are touching, warming and burrowing into one another.

Similar examples of animal-human writing relations are ubiquitous in the everyday and well documented on the internet. While this ubiquity invites uncritical views, my contention is that we can mine these partnerships to better understand the situated nature of writing writ large—in a world populated by all sorts of creatures in both explicit and implicit communion. As my research indicates, writing activities are frequently mediated by the presence of nonhuman others, and once we see this as meaningful, we are primed to consider writing as an overt practice of dwelling with others in the world. Also, animal companions in scenes of writing make visible dual realities of writing: writing is a lonely pursuit and always populated with others.

This chapter deviates from the preceding ones by including results from a qualitative study of animals in composing environments. The first section presents examples from written acknowledgments that demonstrate how nonhuman creatures contribute to writing activities. The remainder of the chapter reports on field research, prompted by my findings in acknowledgments, aimed at showing how writers conceive the contributions that animal companions make to their composing lives. These contributions acknowledge partners that render writing an art of living and engaging with a range of others.

〜〜〜

"On the home front, a number of cats lent a great deal of warmth and a general sense of well-being to the composing process, including the much missed Kitty and Clyde and the current throng consisting of Casey, Gabe, Hansel, and Simon." This is an excerpt from Donna Strickland's acknowledgment in *The Managerial Unconscious*. The cats, as it happens, figure more prominently than her "dearest companion" named in the next brief sentence. In another example, an author of *GenAdmin* moves seamlessly between thanking her coauthors and animal friends: "To my coauthors for making me think and laugh. To Cima and Eva for their furry friendship" (Charlton et al. v). The proximity of the sentences, revealing other forms of physical and felt proximity, suggests that animals are not mere props or background but are intimately intertwined with writing.

Likewise, in *The Teacher's Body: Embodiment, Authority, and Identity in the Academy*, the editors cite the beginning of their collaboration by referring to the meals they made for their "cooperative household of seven students and two dogs" (Freedman and Holmes xv). Collaboration is influenced "by what happens," to borrow from Bukowski, and what happens cannot be traced directly from idea to talk or writing but is messily concocted through a series of interactions, activities, and "outside" contaminants: food, cooking, animals, a co-housing partnership—all of which constitute the scene of invention, not merely a setting or place where writing "took place."

In some cases, if one didn't know better, animal companions could be mistaken for co-authors. They are described as present and dedicated during the writing and linked to the physical work of writing. Take, for instance, Patricia Donahue's mention of dogs in her acknowledgment for *Local Histories*: "The bichon frises, Lily and Isabelle, remained steadfast in their devotion" (xiv). Her like-minded co-editor, Gretchen Flesher Moon, also praises four-legged contributions to the collaboration, "Brisk early morning walks with Fritz and Jeb (dogs of no discernible breed, but of great curiosity) made long days poring over the manuscript physically bearable" (xiv). "Physically bearable" suggests the embodied contributions these dogs make to the writing—perhaps similar to Emily Straub's earlier mention of how her cats keep her physically rooted. "Brisk early morning walks," made necessary by the dogs, starkly contrasts with "long days" of presumed physical stillness spent "poring over the manuscript." In Lee-Ann Kastman Breuch's acknowledgment for *Virtual Peer Review*, she thanks "Holly, for wonderful walks and for being my constant companion during long days at the computer" (x), calling to mind dog companionship, though I cannot be sure about that.

Haraway, who writes about cross-species co-evolution and habitation, unsurprisingly acknowledges dogs in her book *When Species Meet*. In the final paragraph of her acknowledgments, she writes, "How can I acknowledge Cayenne and Roland, the dogs of my heart? This book is for them, even if they might prefer a scratch-and-sniff version, one without endnotes" (x). Her love note reverberates throughout the book, as she explores how partners co-evolve and so, as she writes, "do not precede their relating" (17). On this point, Haraway explains in *The Companion Species Manifesto* that "[t]here are no pre-constituted subjects and objects, and no single sources, unitary actors, or final ends" (6). For her, every form of identification is a "produc[t] of relating"; we know ourselves as subjects, objects, genders, and so forth, only in relation to others (7).

In a similar vein, writing, as documented in acknowledgments, is animated by everything we do, encounter, everything we are when making sense of the world through language. Material structures, technologies and tools, chairs, music, friends, feelings, power grids, tables, forms of physical embodiment, and non-human others. Writing is the product of these and other relations. And relations are the stuff of writing, whether at the syntactic level—how words and sentences express and embody relationships among persons, ideas, things—or the content level—citation practices and the connected role of influence in writing, audience matters, and meaning-making more broadly. Writing is contaminated, made possible by a mingling of forces and energies in diverse environments composed of various partners. The next section illustrates this point as I report on a qualitative study I conducted to complement and expand my analysis of written acknowledgments. Through the study, I sought to understand what sorts of contributions writers in rhetoric and composition would attribute to animals, and what writers would acknowledge as rhetorically, intellectually, emotionally, and/or physically significant about being with animals in scenes of composing. The next section details my methods and results.

STUDYING WRITERS AND THEIR COMPANIONS

"I can't even find a roach to commune with."

– Charles Bukowski, "metamorphosis"

In March 2014 I distributed an electronic survey link via WPA-L, inviting rhetoric and composition specialists to complete a survey on composing with animals. Sixty-one people completed the survey of 11 questions, the first of which immediately limited the respondent pool: "Do you regularly write in spaces shared with animals?" (see Appendix B for survey questions and IRB documentation). The one respondent who answered "no" was directed to exit the survey, as I did not want a general overview of writers and animals. I wanted a more particular view of how those who write in the presence of animals depict and understand that experience. Thus, my findings are not generalizable to a broad swatch of writers in the field; they reflect a small, self-selected sub-set of field members and are shaped by my deliberate limitations on the research design.

I focused on professionals in rhetoric and composition because I wanted to understand how teachers and researchers in a field organized around writing make sense of their own writing partners and environments. A larger, more diverse study sample could offer comparative insights—i.e., how do critical writers in various fields describe partners? What, if any, patterns emerge across and within disciplines?—thereby constructing a more representative account of critical writers at work. My goals for this research, then, are modest and preliminary. I hope the data builds on existing accounts in composition studies of how writers write, including work by Gary Olson and Lynn Worsham, whose edited collection *Critical Intellectuals on Writing* exposes the rituals and writing scenes of transdisciplinary theorists; Leon and Pigg's study of graduate students as accomplished multitaskers; and Waldrep's (now very dated) 1985 and 1987 two-volume collection of essays by researchers in composition studies, *Writers on Writing*.

Respondents to my survey included tenure-line faculty (31%), full time non-tenure-track faculty (41%), and doctoral students (28%). As Chart 4.1 illustrates, the top three forms of writing the respondents most engage in are scholarship, teaching materials, and email. Most of that writing is done in homes (100%), followed by offices (51%) and coffee shops (39%) (note that respondents could select multiple locations).

Q3 Identify the kinds of writing that you regularly engage in (select all that apply):

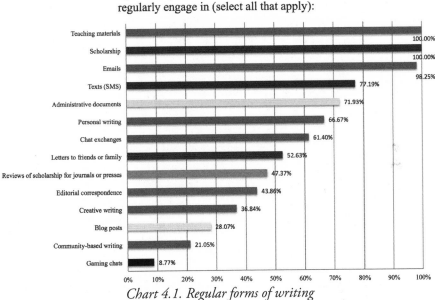

Chart 4.1. Regular forms of writing

A notable outlier, one respondent commented that s/he writes in a truck when taking retreats to the ocean, mountain, or desert, though the writer says nothing about the presence of animals in these settings. I mention it here mostly because the comment made me curious about connections between place, travel, and writing—a subject for another study.

The survey included both closed- and open-ended questions, with much of the substantive data predictably emerging from the latter as well as from the optional Facebook group site, "Composing with Animals," to which survey participants were invited to submit photos depicting the presence of animals in their writing environments. Thirty-two people who completed the survey accepted my invitation to post photos to the Facebook group; half that number ended up joining the group, and ultimately ten participants—one male and nine females—posted material to the site. Instructions for the Facebook group were in part as follows: "Please post photos of animals in your writing environment to this page, and feel free to add commentary. However you interpret 'writing environment' is really up to you" (for a complete description of the group as well as posting instructions, see Appendix C). The 27 postings by 10 participants on the group page span nearly a year—from June 24, 2014 through May 6, 2015. As I write this in May 2016, the group is still open and available to participants even as my research collection process is complete.

In the survey portion of my research, forty-six participants identified animals who are a regular part of their composing environments to be equally divided among dogs and cats (28 participants each), with one rabbit and one bird also selected from my prepared list of options. In the comments section of this question, more diversity surfaced. Writers added the following animal companions:

- Mule deer outside the window
- Coyotes, ravens, and cows ("I mean, they're not in 'my' scene, but we're sharing a space and we know each other are there.")
- Fish ("I had a betta fish that I mostly credit for getting me through my dissertation.")
- Guinea pig and chickens
- Horses ("I have two horses and while they are not present, per se, when I am writing, I often use my time with them to think about and process my work.")

Most respondents answered that two animals populate their writing environments (41%), followed by one (28%), and then three (24%). While I had originally envisioned, without realizing I was doing so, domestic pets as the writing companions who would make appearances in the data, the respondent additions of animals in their wider environments demonstrated that encounters with others are not dependent on proximity or touch (as many of the survey responses cited below tend to underscore). In processing the data, I was reminded of Ingold's point that, when it comes to connections between humans and others, there is no "radical break between social and ecological relations" ("Hunting" 49). In that sense, writing and writers are in the world, not just in the room.

In the most descriptive, qualitative information about the relationship between writers and animal companions, we catch glimpses of what "withness" means to the participants and how those meanings might be linked to acknowledgments: feelings of gratitude, indebtedness, emotional and physical reliance. My discussion of results focuses on responses to questions 8–11, which address, respectively, forms of contact; values animals contribute to the writing process; reflection on the phrasing "writing companion" to describe animals; and, lastly, an open-ended invitation to add other thoughts. Forty-six participants responded to Q8-10, and twenty-three responded to Q11. Collectively, participants created a rich portrait of how writers compose with animals and a range of responses addressing what sense they make of that witchness.

To highlight patterns in the survey responses, I conducted a frequency analysis, coding data segments based on rate of occurrence. Since I designed the study to include only those who write with animals, the data collection process helped me gain more insight about my thesis, which I would characterize as follows: writers write with animals physically or mentally near, and this has some effect on composing. Thus, my reduction of the data for presentation purposes here does not require me to select representative and discrepant samples: all of the data is representative of my originating thesis, an appropriate outcome given that I aim to construct an impressionistic portrait of these writers rather than prove they constitute a preponderance of writers in the field.

The remainder of this chapter is organized by the following categories and subcategories, which constitute my coding scheme (see Appendix D): writing process (perseverance; proximity); communication (modality; effects); writer identity (self-perception; affect). These categories represent themes that emerged with regular frequency in responses to open-ended questions. Participant responses, excerpted below, are presented anonymously in order to make no unnecessary distinctions between those who granted permission to be identified and those who did not. This decision is appropriate given that my emphasis is on descriptions of writing environments rather than writer identity. By working with the respondents' words as is (I made no changes or corrections), I'm able to construct a descriptive account of how writers interpret the role of animals in composing scenes and to connect those accounts to acknowledgments generally—not exclusively the written genre but, more broadly, rhetorical gestures that credit others with meaningful contributions to writing that vary in form and kind.

WRITING PROCESS: PERSEVERANCE AND PROXIMITY

Within the writing process category, participants address activities linked to generating writing. Perseverance, the first subcategory, refers to a writer's ability to persist at writing. The second, proximity, has to do with closeness of animals and writers during writing sessions. Responses in this category suggest that animal companions participate in writing activities in various ways, not merely as "company," a reasonable assumption upon first glance. The participants describe how they persist, day after day, working on complicated projects that can be all consuming and lonely. One respondent, for example, states, "Writing can be lonely, especially because I generally prefer to write alone (I'm wont to talk if I write with others), but writing with a dog cuddled up with me, or even if they are asleep in the same room where I write, can help me to endure and write more." Others addressed the ways in which animals enforced much-needed breaks, helping one writer to "forge ahead and get through the hard parts of writing. [My dogs] also are a welcome break and stress reliever." Recognizing the deleterious effects of over-work, one person notes, "my animals are helping to force a break so that I don't work too long." Perseverance and proximity are explicitly linked by one respondent: "I take great pleasure in patting and playing with [my dog]. In warmer weather, we might go out on the deck. I read; she watches and smells the yard. What is most important, I find, is that she provides friendship, companionship, a feeling not being alone—and I do think that provides me with perseverance."

Correlating to perseverance, when asked to identify values that animals seem to contribute to the writing process, writers largely selected positive values, as Chart 4.2 shows, with comfort, pleasure, and distraction ranking highest.

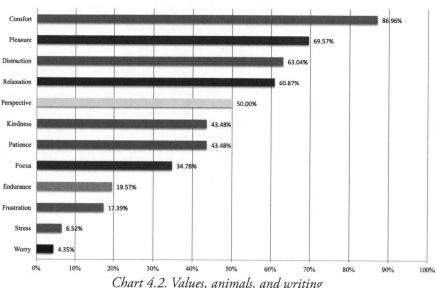

Q9 Identify values that animals seem to contribute to your writing process:

Value	Percentage
Comfort	86.96%
Pleasure	69.57%
Distraction	63.04%
Relaxation	60.87%
Perspective	50.00%
Kindness	43.48%
Patience	43.48%
Focus	34.78%
Endurance	19.57%
Frustration	17.39%
Stress	6.52%
Worry	4.35%

Chart 4.2. Values, animals, and writing

Eleven respondents added other values in the comments, and several explained the positive value of distraction, as did this writer: "I just want to clarify 'distraction'—they distract me away from my computer so I step away from my work momentarily, which often benefits my writing tremendously. I tend to focus on my writing for longer periods of time." This person links "step[ping] away" with overall persistence. Another participant offered "resilience" as a value, which indexes the ability to persist in the face of challenges and/or obstacles. Linking these positive values to writer persistence and to animal need (to play, to walk, etc.), each agent comes to "co-constitute one another" in mutually beneficial ways (Haraway, *When* 4). It's worth noting, however, that sometimes this entanglement, bordering on dependency, can impede progress and adaptability to new circumstances. For example, one respondent confessed, "When we lost our cats last year (3 in four months), I could barely be in the house without them, and I could certainly not write." The effects of companion attachments are not unequivocally comforting.

When asked to identify kinds of contact writers have with animals while writing, participants responded as follows:

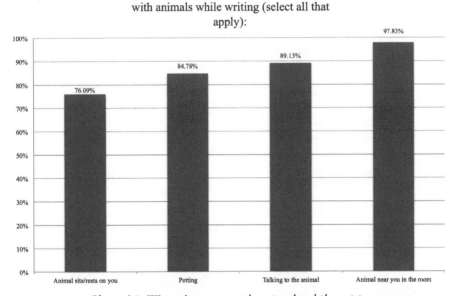

Q8 Explain what kind of contact you have with animals while writing (select all that apply):

Chart 4.3. Writers' contact with animals while writing

Respondents added 20 comments, offering clarifications of "contact" not accounted for in my answer selections. In so doing, contact came to signify play, taking breaks, working out ideas, and sensory experiences. Here's a representative sampling of those responses:

> I attend to their needs when they communicate they have them, such as going outside, or sometimes just wanted my attention (touch).

> I will play with my dog (throwing a ball or tugging on a toy) while I'm working. One of my cat often places his paw on my computer key board while I'm working or if I set my computer down to go into a room for a minute. I often have to go back and erase his "revisions."

> Regularly, my cat initiates play while I am writing. Some
> games require me to stop writing, stand up, and move around
> the room; other games require only that I through something,
> usually kibble.

What might escape notice because seemingly commonplace—walking a dog, writing with cats on our desks—seems crucial to how critical writers accomplish their goals and persist with the competitive, laborious and often lonely task of critical writing. One participant offered this representative sentiment: "I don't know if/how I would write without my cat or cats nearby. I wrote my book and each of my articles with the presence of a cat or cats close by."

Proximity is most often understood as physical closeness by participants of both the survey and the Facebook photo group. Figures 4.9 and 4.10 offer visual and narrative examples that ground much of the commentary cited above.

Figure 4.9: Photo credit: Jenn Fishman.[1]

Proximity, however, is sometimes configured otherwise, not solely in terms of nearness. Katie Ryan's animal companions include, for instance, a marmot, and, as pictured in Figure 4.11, a moose, both of whom she describes as welcome distractions from writing.

---

1   Jenn writes, "My cat, Charlie, was born two years ago in the Gambier, OH, woods. When she was 2 months old, she invited herself to a Kenyon Review Young Writers picnic hosted by friends of mine. Initially they took her in and their daughter named her, but half their household are allergic to cats. When I arrived in Gambier a month later to work on Kenyon Writes, Charlie joined me. Since the keyboard on my very old Mac laptop was no longer working (I typed via a bluetooth keyboard), she was able to take up residence directly in front of the screen. For the rest of the summer, she mainly slept while I read a great deal, took lots of notes, and finished the Year 2 IRB along with two article manuscripts."

Figure 4.10: Photo credit: April Conway.[2]

Figure 4.11: Photo credit: Katie Ryan.[3]

---

2   April writes, "My composing companions are my dogs, Paco and Lola. Lola will lay at my feet when I write at the desk upstairs, and sometimes Paco will join her. Similarly, Lola will cuddle right next to me on the bed or couch when I read for my writing, and Paco will join us when he feels like it. My primary writing space, though, is at the dining room table, and so most often my view, when I look up from the computer, is of Paco and Lola napping in their respective spots on the living room furniture."

3   Katie writes, "Here's my animal neighbor composing distraction of the day. His rear end is over 5 feet tall. A glorious distraction!"

Likewise, Laura Rogers addresses the value of riding her horse as a strategy for getting focused. Riding seems to have a meditative effect on her, helping her to be in the moment which in turn serves her writing (see Figure 4.12).

Figure 4.12: Photo credit: Laura Rogers.[4]

COMMUNICATION: MODALITY AND EFFECTS

As participants reflected on the aptness of "writing companions" to describe their experiences writing with animals, they addressed modes and effects of communication that foregrounded the interactive aspects of their relationships. For example, the sensory modality of sound came up several times. One respondent referred to "purring mixing with the click of keys" as "one of the happiest sounds"; another wrote that listening to dogs snoring was the "best background noise ever!" Others recalled "talking out loud and think[ing] through writing" with cats, or "'writing aloud'" while walking dogs, who are identified as "receptive and non-judgmental listeners" by one participant. While talking to her dog all day, one respondent also benefits from the "feel of her [dog's] fur (especially her super soft ears!) on my fingers when I'm thinking." In another scene of animal contact while writing, a Facebook participant reflects on her cat's role as a "particular kind of actor and interactor," explaining that "much of the time she opts to be/sleep wherever I am working (bed, living room, dining room, kitchen), and when she is awake it's not unusual for her to ask for attention via a paw poking around the side of the computer screen, a paw to the side of my face, a swat to the legs followed by a dash across the room, and so on." This respondent "value[s] and enjoy[s]" this kind of interactivity.

Tactile and sensory communication have clear effects on writers and writing. Responses focused on altered affective, mental, or physical states; renewed or

---

4   Laura writes, "While my Morgan mare Jessie is not part of my immediate composing environment, she is an important part of my writing process. Riding/being with a horse requires that one be totally in the present moment . . . I can return to writing more focused, present and grounded."

depleted energy for writing; and changed perspectives on writing. For example, one respondent noted that "my writing days influence [my cat's] experience of the world as much as her presence influences my experience of writing." Another commented, "I see my cat as a companion in the sense that she is often a (loud) verbal reminder of the world around me." Articulating a point made by many, one writer notes that an important effect of animal companions is that they "mak[e] me STOP writing or sitting at my desk. At 4:00 p.m., they're letting me know it's time for our afternoon walk, and I think that's as important as anything else." Sometimes the cohabitation becomes so intertwined that writers alter their writing lives to align with the lives of animals in their midst. In this vein, one writer describes her relationship with her ailing dog as a "mutual dependency," which "became so intense that when I moved to my first job post-graduation, I was very reluctant to leave home to work at my office. . . . My dog (in concert with my research) changed my relationship to writing and to my attachment to public settings when I write."

IDENTITY: SELF-PERCEPTION AND AFFECT

Self-efficacy, confidence, and self-worth emerged as values writers frequently attached to their experiences with animal companions. Often their comments came up in the context of writing as a lonely activity (i.e., writing with pets near-by "alleviates loneliness of writing"). One respondent notes that having a dog at one's feet while writing makes "you feel like you have someone who is always cheering for you"—though she is quick to point out that this feeling does not necessarily extend to cats, who are likely to make her feel "like I am always being silently judged," calling to mind Hemingway's comment on how a cat does not hide her feelings. Another writer gains great comfort and presence of mind from a dog's nearness when "feeling desperate" about writing. Noting that the dog "has been beside me for every book I've read, every piece I've written, every presentation I've made, and every class I've taught," the writer reveals something of the psychic difficulty of writing and the contributions her dog makes to easing that difficulty: "She reminds me, especially in the long dark hours of night writing, that we've 'done it' and we'll 'do it' again! When the voices in my head get to be too loud and I feel as though I'm losing my mind, she has a calming and mind-clearing effect."

This sentiment was articulated in numerous ways by participants. One says her dog companion generates "inspiration and centeredness," reminding her of "my sense of purpose." Regular contact with a dog improves another participant's self-worth: "Seeing how much my dog utterly adores me—even when my writing is awful—reminds me that I'm more than a 'writer' or a 'professor.'"

Here we venture into issues of identity and the construction of self through contact with the other. This comment also addresses the value of a widened perspective while writing—lightening the weight of writing by situating it in a broader field of activity where other responsibilities and pleasures are located—a point echoed by countless respondents. Another simply states, "Pet presence and contentment offset my own frustrations."

These excerpts highlight the value of animals as loyal companions who offer a concentrated sense of calm and rootedness in a reality that is not dependent on academic work to validate worth or goodness. Given the difficult emotional labor associated with writing, as we saw in chapter two, a reminder of one's value beyond the human centered endeavor of academic work acts as a reprieve, an important grounding in the material world and corresponding cohabitation in it. The acknowledgments of animal contributions to the daily work of writing are simultaneously earthly and transcendent, as they offer a peek into writing spaces grounded in mundane relations between writers and animals while also highlighting the complex psychological state of writers who, in appreciating re-spite from loneliness, doubt, and anxiety, often attribute their ability to tran-scend the hard production of writing to animal companions.

Or sometimes transcendence is not the goal. Sometimes identity as a writer, teacher, and person are so intimately tied to animals that the partnership is com-plete. Examples in this vein emerged in the Facebook group, where participants (understandably) revealed more about their lives than did survey participants, as they shared glimpses of their writing worlds through photos. We see not only animals in writing scenes but also personal spaces dense with the stuff of writing (computers, pencils, books, papers, coffee cups, etc.) and with life around writ-ing (dishes, windows, rugs, couches, decorations, outdoor settings, lamps, etc.). I've come to think of the Facebook contributions as portraits-in-miniature of what the survey data suggests. They add texture and intimacy to the overall data.

Connecting writing and life in a striking way, one Facebook contributor writes:

> I don't have children so I don't know what it must be like to think about my child incessantly but I do have dogs and I do think about my dogs incessantly, particularly when they are in pain and need my care. Work has been something that has to fall by the wayside when they need my attention but has also been a haven to expel all of my worry/anxiety ridden energies. Sam's disabilities have made me more mindful of disability studies and it has in turn affected the way I see the world and think about Composition pedagogy and practice.

This excerpt is one of few in my research that explicitly addresses the interactive relationship between animal companionship and disciplinary concerns, reminding me of Haraway's *The Companion Species Manifesto*, in which she argues that humans and dogs "shape each other" (29) and are "products of their relating" (7).

REFLECTING ON THE DWELT-IN WORLD

"Environments are constituted in life, not just in thought, and it is only because we live in an environment that we can think at all," writes Ingold ("Hunting" 50). This claim clicked for me when I read through and processed the data for this study. I could not shake the idea that my respondents had set out to convince me that a writing environment is not so much about creating a space in which we can articulate our thoughts as much as it is about creating a dwelling where writing is just one activity interacting with others. In other words, the interaction and diversity is what really seems to matter to the participants of the survey and the Facebook group page. These writers encourage us to consider writing as always part of the dwelt-in world, and so to consider it apart from its habitats, as inevitably happens when we make writing teachable, when we give it the textbook treatment, is to mangle writing's lived qualities. I'm not sure there's any way around this, but it bears noticing that writing theory and practice must continually evolve, remain ever awake to more of the surround and eager to grow through interaction with it.

In practical terms, the takeaway of this chapter isn't that composition courses should be conducted with animals present (though that sounds good to me) or that theory must always account for how living creatures, beyond humans, bear on writing activity. Rather, my hope is that this study of animals and composers encourages teachers and scholars to insist on writing environments as central to what makes writing possible. More importantly, I believe this research speaks to embodied, sensory-rich, and cognitive studies of pedagogy and rhetoric that emphasize difference as key to appreciating the many variables that inflect writing activities. As such, thinking of and with animals generates questions about moral and psychological connections between self and other, what it means to be writing animals ourselves, and operative constructions of identity (what do they include? Exclude? What are the boundaries between self and other? How do bodies and identities blur together? What are the effects?). In other words, I see the study in this chapter as interfacing with broader efforts to pose questions about identity and difference that have bearing on writing activities so that these categories are not presumed or taken for granted. In addition, the accumulated study of acknowledgments throughout this book and the emphasis on varied partnerships develop a wide frame of reference for collaboration. What contributes to school writing activity is both plain to see (assignments, peers, teachers, tutors, technology, etc.) and embedded in diverse contexts of activity (feeling, time, animal company).

The presence of animals in scenes of composing makes explicit the dialectic of writing as a lonely pursuit and writing as always collaborative. Through partnerships of various kinds with animals, writers are changed, even if only temporarily when a mood lifts and confidence returns. This claim expands my study of written acknowledgments so that acknowledging more generally might be theorized as central to the work of writing writ large. We are always dependent on others, learning from them, being changed by and changing in response to others, and finding our way through and with language while occupying scenes of cross-species (and other) partnerships.

CONCLUSION
MANGLE OF PRACTICE

How writing happens, how small increments of language come to be something larger, will probably always remain at least partly elusive. We can study key strokes, writing logs, writing protocol responses, final products, real-time observations of writers in action, writers' reflections on their processes, final reflections, eye-tracking results, neurological data, screen captures and videos of writers writing, among other data points that tell partial stories about writing. Still, a comprehensive understanding of the life cycle of writing, its production and its affective triggers, lies perpetually beyond our grasp. This is because the complexity of writing is both commonplace and extraordinary.

Rather than signaling the impossibility of writing research, however, perpetually incomplete writing studies gesture to the exuberant vitality of writing activity; no matter our best efforts, it cannot be pinned down. In the absence of comprehensive accounts of writing, we can monitor and document what scientist Andrew Pickering calls the "mangle of practice." For Pickering, science is characterized by a set of ongoing interactions between people and things, humans and nonhumans. Science, he contends, is best understood as a "dance of agency" (78). In this dance, a scientist is "trying this, seeing what happens, trying something else" (81). As an example, Pickering discusses an experiment with a bubble chamber, also known as a radiation detector, conducted by Donald Glaser that involved a series of recursive moves. "Sometimes Glaser acted as a classical human agent; then he would become passive and the apparatus took over the active role, doing its thing; then Glaser took over again, back and forth; and eventually a working bubble chamber emerged at the end" (Pickering 78).

Glaser's process and his engagement with the environment is performative, as Pickering points out (78), meaning that his observations, adjustments, and contributions responded to collaborations with his materials and emerged from an authentic situation. Glaser's process illustrates a refusal to "edit out the emergent aspects of the dance by substituting scientific representations for them" (Pickering 81). This is important. The dance of agency, for Pickering, represents a way of doing science that stays connected to the world. In contrast, he explains, "Scientific experiment depends on the detour I have been talking about: a displacement of phenomena away from the world and into the lab for the sake of producing knowledge which can then be re-exported to the world . . . " (81). That "we usually contrive not to see" the "emergent aspects of the dance" (81) has significance for knowledge making activities of all kinds, including those within writing studies. Can we, should we, conduct studies of writing by participating in and documenting "[c]onstant monitoring of worldly performance" as itself part of what's worth knowing (82)? Pickering's point about worldly performance is not that monitoring activity can "ever pi[n] down the actual complexities of any important real ecosystem," but that we "simply have to look" in order to see the world and its activity as "lively and surprising" (83).

This book constitutes an effort to document the mangle of writing practice as represented by writers in the afterglow of writing's completion. It is an attempt to document the dance of agency that writers describe in acknowledgments, not with the goal of figuring out once and for all what conditions make critical, scholarly work possible, but with intent to foreground the emergent aspects of writing—borrowing a book from a friend, writing alongside animals, being affected by personal and/or political realities that change the shape of a project, and so forth. While my study lacks real-time observation of writers in motion, it does highlight how writers tell stories about writing. Implicitly, then, *Acknowledging Writing Partners* values narrative choices—not narrative veracity—as indicators of perceived as well as tacitly coerced writing debts performed within the context of acknowledgments. The book also highlights how a micro view of composing is valuable and can complement larger scale studies of writing and cultural identity. Further, despite a widespread immunity to focusing on individuals (and thereby the humanist subject), *Acknowledging Writing Partners* foregrounds individual and collective representations of writing and writers as sources that have relevance to writing pedagogy.

The individual-collective dialectic was animated for me today by a philosophy student in a dissertation writing class that I'm currently teaching. She wanted to know how I get writing done in between other responsibilities within and outside academia. "It helps to hear how people do this work," she confided. "Even though I know everyone's process is different, I just want to know what it's like for other writers." I share this student's interest and, ultimately, desire to feel less alone in the pursuit of putting words together because her comments resonate with Pickering's description of what it means to understand science. He argues that one first needs to know "(a) the performance of scientists—what scientists do; (b) the performance of the material world . . .; and (c) how those performances are interlaced with one another" (78). He views the "performative struggles" between the human and material world to be the central content of science (78). The take-away from *Acknowledging Writing Partners* is analogous to Pickering's point in that my reading of acknowledgments reveals writers' documentations of "performative struggles" and of relationships between writer and material world. In short, knowing how writers tell the story of writing is knowing something about writing. The graduate student who asked about my writing process seemed to understand this intuitively.

I hope this book generates a change in thinking and vocabulary from "writing about" to "writing with" to reflect that partnerships abound in relation to writing activity. Writing is inconceivable outside partnerships, by which I mean something more than the idea that writing is collaborative: practiced with other people, and in response to feedback (though, obviously, both are true, and both are collaborative). Writing is populated and partnered in ways that we can't always recognize. An indiscreet art, writing is something we do with others, created through contact with and exposure to diverse influences and agents. The fabric on your favorite chair, the smell of the laundromat down the street, the light coming in through a window, the muffled voices half heard through floorboards, the cat on your lap—all of these partners make writing a thoroughly collaborative—COLLABORATIVE!—event. I believe that awareness of this expansive view of collaboration, understood as involvement in and with the world, generates sensitivity to diverse writing practices as well as nurtures curiosity about writing, revealing the extent to which writing encompasses so much that we do not yet know or understand. Learning how to "simply. . . look," as Pickering puts it, can lead to revelations of writing's strangeness and stimulate grounds for further research inspired by emergent aspects of writing and the "dance of agency" characteristic of its production.

Of course, "simply looking" is not really so simple. How do we look? Through what lens? With what kind of attention? My study suggests that "looking" can benefit from more roaming, more lack of direction so that we can discover usable insights from interdisciplinary research and/or come to view accidental or mundane encounters as potentially promising content for intellectual work. Learning to appreciate the vitality of seemingly disconnected attachments can bloom into something substantial—for me, in this study, such attachments include a good album, a stirring acknowledgment, Lynda Barry on pedagogy, social media's obsession with animals and writers, Karl Ove Knaussgard, texts I happen to be teaching. Within composition studies, Ann Berthoff persistently models this approach to research and writing. Her edited collection, *Reclaiming the Imagination: Philosophical Perspectives for Writers and Teachers of Writing*, is practically a how-to guide for widening one's palette as a thinker and writer. The book includes no readings that directly address teaching writing but instead brings together work by philosophers, scientists, artists, poets, and rhetoricians in order to stimulate imaginative thinking about teaching. Aimed at cultivating a "tolerance for ambiguity" (viii), Berthoff's selections are meant to instigate thought rather than "cover" the topic of imagination. I recently stumbled upon another version of this approach to writing in a book called *How to Write About*

Music, edited by Marc Woolworth and Ally-Jane Grossan. In preparation for writing about a song, the editors coach writers to do the following:

> Research widely and eccentrically about the time and place
> from which the song comes and make a list of ten facts,
> events, and phenomena of that moment and locale that do
> not have anything directly to do with the song, the artist, or
> music in general. See what's happening in areas as distinct as
> philosophy, fashion, medicine, politics, and law—anything
> can prove a trigger. Make this list by relying on your intu-
> ition rather than attempting to link up the song in a logical
> way with the elements you choose. Don't despair at this
> point if you can't see a connection between the song and the
> facts. (364)

In reading and writing about acknowledgments, I have tried to follow paths as I've crossed them, allowing eccentricity and interest to guide my attention. I see this book in some ways, then, as an experiment in reading as wandering and making oneself highly suggestible. This stance is consistent with my claim that reading and writing embody a radical withness.

Radical withness, aptly aligned with Pickering's dance of agency, reveals that acknowledgments are rife with unusual (and mundane) details, making them potentially rich sites for writing research as well as for writing assignments. In *Rewriting*, Harris notes that he asks students to compose acknowledgments be-cause they emphasize the labor of writing and the involvement of others in that labor: "Writing is real labor. It requires real time and resources to research, read, draft, revise, and prepare the final copy of a text. And this material work of writing, of the making of texts, almost always involves the help of others" (95). As this study has shown, paying attention to acknowledgments can heighten consciousness of relationships, places, feelings, and a wide array of activities rel-evant to writing—in fact, the curatorial, distributed, and immersed qualities of writing cited in the introduction are no small part of why acknowledgments can be difficult to compose and to consume.

As this study draws to a close, I would be remiss if I failed to mention that ac-knowledgments, however, are but one paratext of a larger genre set of marginal, fringe, or threshold texts that have the capacity to depict writing's constituting qualities. We see intriguing ways to gauge influences and interacting concepts, figures and objects central to writing not only in acknowledgments but also in forewords, epigraphs, footnotes, indexes, works cited, and appendices. Digital paratexts, too, generate expansive vistas through which to view partnerships. I think here, for instance, of Johndan Johnson-Eilola's description of writers and their production informed by virtual composing practices: "[W]riters are not individuals (or even groups) who produce texts, but participants within spaces who are recursively, continually, restructuring those (and other) spaces" (1).

In this light, writers build spaces together online, and one of the ways they do so is through the use of paratexts. Multi-user tagging, for example, constructs organizational schemes that enhance findability and create shared connections otherwise impossible to realize. Pinterest operates on this principle by allowing users to create boards and tags that connect, say, vegetarian food pins to those assembled by other users. Co-constructing space through tagging and creating boards—that is, through writing—is a mode of invention and a tool for materializing community. Because user content on Pinterest is both main and marginal (i.e., some users may follow your vegetarian board; others may never come across it because it lies outside their interest), we can think of tagging and pinning as paratextual genre activities. Jodie Nicotra, who describes multi-user tagging through the term "folksonomy," contends that crafting participatory online spaces refigures concepts of text, agency, and audience traditionally tied to print forms: "With folksonomy, rhetorical agency and intention become much more complicated, because invention is revealed as not simply the product of an individual, isolated mind, but as a distributed process driven by the interaction of a multitude of users. It becomes impossible to assign the origins of the invention to any one individual; rather, invention emerges from a crowd" (W273). Thus, folksonomy—made up of paratextual components—is "nondirectional, bottom-up" collective writing (W273).

Digital writing partnerships are varied, dynamic, and increasingly central to participatory, crowd-sourced virtual community and meaning-making activities. Such partnerships reveal different kinds of information about writing than does my study of acknowledgments, largely concentrated on writing debts of one kind or another. Like acknowledgments, though, digital paratexts widen our view of what we can say about writing as a communal practice, an activity never without partners. Paratexts make center and margins perceptible, even if their distinctions become blurred; and awareness of writing partnerships admits diverse actants into the activity of writing. This matters because writing might be taught with more bodily awareness than it is currently, framing writing as a holistic practice that entails body, others, materials, and environment. Even just making this idea speakable could contribute to a more elastic culture of writing, one that encourages an approach to writing instruction built not only from what students know and need to know about writing skills but also from physiological, social, biological, and material experiences that contextualize knowing. Who or what is in charge of writing a research paper, for instance? The writer, library, the sources, the assignment, the tools and materials, the access, the place where you encounter the research? While we often talk about rhetoric as relational and contextual, acknowledgments illustrate these principles very well for us and our students. We might use such texts as a basis for teaching writing practices, as well as for asking students to construct their own project-based narratives. What kinds of dances with agency are students doing and what are the implications for writing pedagogy and theory?

POSTSCRIPT

"Most of what I know about writing I've learned through running every day."

> – Haruki Murakami, *What I Talk about When I Talk About Running*

Haruki Murakami's memoir on writing and running is written with enigmatic, sometimes off-putting matter-of-factness. For instance, he states, "Emotional hurt is the price a person has to pay in order to be independent" (19). And again, "I don't think most people would like my personality. There might be a few—*very* few, I would imagine—who are impressed by it, but only rarely would anyone like it" (20–21). He closes the book with a proposal for his gravestone:

Haruki Murakami
1949–20**
Writer (and Runner)
At Least He Never Walked (174)

Aside from revealing the author's slightly awkward yet charming character, the book explores the central role of running to Murakami's writing process. Running clears mental space, creating a "void" during which he doesn't think "much of anything worth mentioning" (17). And running provides a means for relieving dissatisfaction and bad feelings, which simultaneously makes him "realize again how weak I am, how limited my abilities are. I become aware, physically, of these low points" (20). He runs "in order to acquire a void," not to work out ideas for his novels, as convention might dictate. Only occasionally, he confides, does he "get an idea to use in a novel" while running (17). And yet, creating the void is preparation for writing, as it quiets his mind and generates calm and receptivity to language, story, and the immediate environment. Emptying his mind (as much as possible), not filling it up, is for Murakami a desirable precondition for writing. Putting it another way in an interview with *The Paris Review*, Murakami describes the repetition of his writing rituals as a "form of mesmerism" aimed at reaching a "deeper state of mind," reminding me of Perl's felt sense.

Murakami's comments suggest that elements outside the writer and outside writing-proper are not only important to the production of writing but also constitute writing activity itself. Writing scholar Barbara Tomlinson articulates a similar point when she says that writing "is not a discrete event, but a pattern, a background of repetitive moves, ways of thinking, ways of living" (35). Written acknowledgments in academic texts often confirm this point, though, as we saw in chapter one, they are typically interpreted, on the one hand, as evidence of the social scene of writing, and, on the other, as trite performatives, ripe for parody and dismissal. In contrast, for me, what writers see fit to thank reveals writing worlds that provide compelling, under-represented accounts of writing practices.

Acknowledgments invoke relationships and, in some cases, power relations. We can see this, for example, in the "Best Acknowledgments" competition, created by Margaret Heilbrun in 2011 and sponsored by *Library Journal*, which highlights, among other things, the labor of knowledge production. She reviews current books by historians and biographers, books that she finds most often entail library research, for acknowledgment of individual librarian contributions to research projects. Authors who thank librarians by name in their acknowledgments are most highly ranked, while the lower ranks include those who thank unnamed librarians at a particular library, interlibrary loan services generally, or, interestingly given my focus in this book, the architecture of a reading room or some other atmospheric. "Librarians, like all mortals," writes Heilbrun, "love to be on the receiving end of gratitude." The 2011 winner, Amanda Foreman, actually became the namesake for a category of acknowledgment in the 2012 competition; the most recent winner follows the Foreman "format" of naming every library accessed and every staff person consulted. The other category of acknowledgments included in the competition is Acknowledgments as Memoir, a personal narrative that includes "the names of all the kind souls in libraries . . . who helped." The award is half tongue-in-cheek, half righteous comeuppance for all the overlooked librarians out there who have contributed in small and large ways to research projects.

The competition for appropriate forms of gratitude makes explicit the value of what acknowledgments often do very well: make elements of composing visible, offering antidotes to abstract conceptions that, wittingly or not, treat writing as interiority externalized. In an early essay about her own writing process, Susan Miller describes the value of composing studies as such: "I think it is very important for those of us who teach to understand what is at stake in our views of composing. [Composing] can itself be elevated and mystified to innocently recreate ideologies we would rather avoid" ("Rebelling" 174–75). The stakes for understanding composing as a complex act that is not merely skill-based are very high, as standardized testing continues to flourish in elementary and secondary education, and as postsecondary writing requirements are increasingly being eroded by dual-enrollment and other credit-granting programs that waive students from taking first-year writing (see Hansen and Farris). While my project is not a direct intervention into state-sanctioned assessment of college student writing, I believe studies of composing that expose its complexity can counter misperceptions that writing is only as complex as a paragraph response to a test question. Against such simplifications, this book argues through a study of acknowledgments that writing is habituated attention to language made possible by the conditions and others that surround it.

I began this project by stating that I do not worry over distinctions between truth and fiction in acknowledgments, as both are rhetorical acts of choice-making that reveal worlds of writing. In homage to that commitment, I end with an exquisite corpse of acknowledgments excerpts, authored by the many partners I encountered during the drafting of this book and strung together to create a Frankensteinian performance of the genre. Because acknowledgments express a great deal of vitality around writing, much of which exceeds the constraints of the preceding chapters, I put that virtue into play, dramatizing the idea that writing is a populated act that has compelling lifecycles. In addition, I felt that ending with others' words, memories, and experiences was the appropriate choice for a book devoted to partners.

~ ~ ~

"And, as a good deal of this book was conceived and written on board a number of fishing and dive boats, we wish to thank all of those boat captains who told us to quit talking about discourse and either get in the water or reel in a fish."[1]

"This book has been a good friend to me in various hospital and hospice rooms, through some very long nights and gloomy sunrises. I say this not to court any forgiveness or lowered expectations, but simply as a way of acknowledging that my father's elegant courage and pervasive desire to be useful inspired me to press on."[2]

"I must also thank my yoga teachers who provided spirit, fortitude (without struggle), and, of course, the breath one cannot do without."[3]

"The beginning of my journey on this book can be traced back to a hike in the Alaskan wilderness outside of Juneau, where friends and I were on our way to a remote cabin."[4]

"Although the result [of my messy writing process] is a decorator's disaster, I know exactly where everything is—all around me like an embrace, exactly where I need it. If the authors of these works were here in person the room would look like a CCCC convention, enlivened by a swirl of teachers and writers great and good, philosophers, psychologists, rhetoricians, travelers, social commentators, anthropologists, and more, and student writers, generations past and present. I would great them with the hugs of welcome, and of thanks, that I extend figuratively not only from this page, but on every page of *Composition Studies as a Creative Art.*"[5]

"I wrote much of this book during my wife's terminal illness."[6]

"Finally and with love, I offer special thanks to Isaac Kramnick, who read this manuscript in its entirety on the beaches of Croix-Val-Mer and then again alongside Kelm Lake, acts of sublime virtue beyond the imaginings of any rhetorician."[7]

"To Robb Jackson who kept telling me to just poop it on out. . . .To my daughter Christine and her classmates for teaching me about the disruptive discourse of farting in a sixth-grade classroom."[8]

"Janette Miller, although deceased, somehow still helped me get home—a place I wouldn't know I needed to be otherwise, which I'm grateful for every day."[9]

This book took form through conversations during "conference hotel breakfasts or stolen in those rare moments when our (combined) four children were somehow not needing attention."[10]

"I have depended on a network of scholars, texts, computer hardware and software, friends and family. The entire process has been distributed among countless interactions with people and resources in the environment; it is embodied in this text and in physical interactions with it; it has emerged over time from a few key concepts into a theoretical framework and finally into this extended study; and it has been enacted in a set of practices and activities that range from taking notes in an archive or participating in a lab discussion to formal institutional processes of admission to a discipline."[11]

"This book is the effect of a fortuitous assemblage of friends, colleagues, interlocutors, and other things."[12]

"When Rick died, he had nearly completed this, his fourth book dealing with response to student writing. In fact, several days after his death I received drafts of its introduction and the chapter that we were to write together about *Twelve Readers*, along with a note saying that he looked forward to my responses to each piece. My responses will have to stand as the final word since Rick left us before he could receive them. However, had he lived, those responses would have been only the beginning of our conversation about what the final product should be. To Rick, that's what a teacher's (or anyone's) response should be: the beginning of a conversation. How I wish he had lived to continue that conversation with me!"[13]

"He would be remiss if he did not also mention Michelle Worley and the other bartenders at The Cooker, who always poured him a mean cocktail when he needed one."[14]

"The seed essay for this book, 'In the House of Doing,' was written in 2004 while I was on prednisone for an allergic reaction, and oddly, in 2012, at project's end, I find myself again on prednisone."[15]

"For nearly two years we wrestled with the issues and with ways to present our theories and our findings. I'm sure there were times when I became overbearing, when the authors' temptation to snip the phone cord was enticing, delicious. But no one did."[16]

"Kennan Ferguson has known me since I was nineteen years old, when I used to stomp around and say things like 'Theory is crap.' I cannot thank him enough for his companionship and support over decades."[17]

"My wife, Colleen Connors, did not type or proofread a word of this book. But she knows who made it possible."[18]

"Happily unmarried, I am grateful to my students and colleagues who don't let me get by with much without challenging me."[19]

"Some of my best intellectual inspiration comes from my friends outside academia and the creative worlds that they have built."[20]

NOTES

1. Dobrin and Weisser vii.
2. Lynn xi.
3. Feldman x.
4. Breuch ix.
5. Bloom, *Composition* ix.
6. Berman xi.
7. Brody xii.
8. Bryant xiii.
9. Rohan xii (in Kirsch and Rohan).
10. Haas xvii
11. Syverson xix.
12. Bennett xxi.
13. Lunsford xii.
14. Thelin v (in Tassoni and Thelin).
15. Rickert xxii.
16. Rose xii–xiii.
17. Price vi.
18. Connors x (*Composition-Rhetoric*).
19. Appleby ix (in McCracken and Appleby).
20. Cvetkovich x.

WORKS CITED

"Achilles." *Pets on Academia*, 12 Feb. 2014, petsonacademia.tumblr.com/post/764390
92968/achilles-thinks-my-dissertation-draft-makes-an.

Adler-Kassner, Linda. *The Activist WPA: Changing Stories about Writing and Writers*.
Utah SUP, 2008.

Ahmed, Sara. *On Being Included: Racism and Diversity in Institutional Life*. Duke UP, 2012.

———. "Orientations Matter." *New Materialisms: Ontology, Agency, and Politics*, edited
by Diana Coole and Samantha Frost, Duke UP, 2010, pp. 234–57.

———. *The Promise of Happiness*. Duke UP, 2010.

Alaimo, Stacy, and Susan Hekman, editors. *Material Feminisms*. Indiana UP, 2008.

Alcaraz, María Ángeles. "Acknowledgments in Neurology Research Articles: A Contrastive Study (English-Spanish)." *Fachsprache*, vol. 36, no. 3–4, 2014, pp. 115–27,
www.fachsprache.net/upload/Articles/Alcaraz_Acknowledgments_in_Neurology
_research_articles_3-4_2014.pdf.

Alexander, Jonathan, Laura R. Micciche, and Jacqueline Rhodes. "Indirection, Anxiety,
and the Folds of Reading." *Reader*, no. 65–66, pp. 43–71.

Asia, Daniel. "The Put on of the Century, or the Cage Centenary." *Huffington Post*, 3
Jan. 2013, www.huffingtonpost.com/daniel-asia/the-put-on-of-the-century_b
_2403915.html.

Bakhtin, Mikhail. *The Dialogic Imagination: Four Essays*. Edited by Michael Holquist,
translated by Caryl Emerson and Michael Holquist, U of Texas Press, 1981.

Banks, Adam J. *Race, Rhetoric, and Technology: Searching for Higher Ground*. Lawrence
Erlbaum Associates and National Council of Teachers of English, 2006.

Baron, Dennis. *A Better Pencil: Readers, Writers, and the Digital Revolution*. Oxford UP,
2009.

Barry, Lynda. *Syllabus: Notes from an Accidental Professor*. Drawn & Quarterly, 2014.

Barthes, Roland. "The Death of the Author." *Image / Music / Text*, translated by Ste-
phen Heath, Hill and Wang, 1977, pp. 142–47.

Bartholomae, David. "Against the Grain." Waldrep, pp. 19–29.

———. "Living in Style." Bartholomae, *Writing*, pp. 1–16.

———. *Writing on the Margins: Essays on Composition and Teaching*. Bedford/St.
Martin's, 2004.

Bawarshi, Anis S. *Genre and the Invention of the Writer: Reconsidering the Place of Invention in Composition*. Utah SUP, 2003.

Belanoff, Pat, and Marcia Dickson, editors. *Portfolios: Process and Product*. Boynton/
Cook, 1991.

Ben-Ari, Eyal. "On Acknowledgements in Ethnographies." *Journal of Anthropological
Research*, vol. 43, no. 1, 1987, pp. 63–84, doi: 10.1086/jar.43.1.3630467.

Benesch, Sarah. *Considering Emotions in Critical English Language Teaching: Theories
and Praxis*. Routledge, 2012.

Bennett, Jane. *Vibrant Matter: A Political Ecology of Things*. Duke UP, 2010.

Berlin, James A. *Rhetoric and Reality: Writing Instruction in American Colleges, 1900–1985*. Southern Illinois UP, 1987.

Berman, Jeffrey. *Empathic Teaching: Education for Life*. U of Massachusetts P, 2004.

Berry, Theodorea Regina, and Nathalie Mizelle, editors. *From Oppression to Grace: Women of Color and Their Dilemmas within the Academy*. Stylus Publishing, 2006.

Berthoff, Ann E. *Forming/Thinking/Writing: The Composing Imagination*. Hayden Book Company, 1978.

———, with James Stephens. *Forming/Thinking/Writing*. 2nd ed., Boynton/Cook, 1988.

———, editor. *Reclaiming the Imagination: Philosophical Perspectives for Writers and Teachers of Writing*. Boynton/Cook, 1984.

Bloom, Lynn Z. *Composition Studies as a Creative Art: Teaching, Writing, Scholarship, Administration*. Utah State UP, 1998.

———. "How I Write." Waldrep, pp. 31–37.

Boice, Robert. *Professors as Writers: A Self-Help Guide to Productive Writing*. New Forums, 1990.

Boler, Megan. *Feeling Power: Emotions and Education*. Routledge, 1999.

Brande, Dorothea. *Becoming a Writer*. 1934. Tarcher/Putnam, 1981.

Brent, Harry. "Epistemological Presumptions in the Writing Process." Waldrep, pp. 45–61.

Breuch, Lee-Ann Kastman. *Virtual Peer Review: Teaching and Learning about Writing in Online Environments*. SUNY P, 2004.

Brodkey, Linda. *Academic Writing as Social Practice*. Temple UP, 1987.

———. *Writing Permitted in Designated Areas Only*. U of Minnesota P, 1996.

Brody, Miriam. *Manly Writing: Gender, Rhetoric, and the Rise of Composition*. Southern Illinois UP, 1993.

Bryant, Lizbeth A. *Voice as Process*. Boynton/Cook, 2005.

Buchanan, Brett. "Being with Animals: Reconsidering Heidegger's Animal Ontology." Gross and Vallely, pp. 265–88.

Bukowski, Charles. "The History of a Tough Motherfucker." Bukowski, pp. 455–57.

———. "Metamorphosis." Bukowski, pp. 14.

———. *The Pleasures of the Damned: Poems, 1951–1993*. Edited by John Martin, HarperCollins, 2007.

Bullock, Richard, and John Trimbur, editors. *The Politics of Writing Instruction: Postsecondary*. Boynton/Cook, 1991.

Caesar, Terry. "On Acknowledgements." *The New Orleans Review*, vol. 19, no. 1, 1992, pp. 85–94.

Canagarajah, A. Suresh. *A Geopolitics of Academic Writing*. U of Pittsburgh P, 2002.

———. *Translingual Practice: Global Englishes and Cosmopolitan Relations*. Routledge, 2013.

Carr, Nicholas. *The Shallows: What the Internet is Doing to Our Brains*. W. W. Norton, 2011.

Charlton, Colin, Jonikka Charlton, Tarez Samra Graban, Kathleen J. Ryan, and Amy Ferdinandt Stolley. *GenAdmin: Theorizing WPA Identities in the Twenty-First Century*. Parlor P, 2011.

Clark, Andy. *Being There: Putting Brain, Body, and World Together Again.* MIT P, 1997.

Coen, Joel, and Ethan Coen, directors. *Barton Fink.* Circle Films, 1991.

Connors, Robert J. *Composition-Rhetoric: Backgrounds, Theory, and Pedagogy.* U of Pittsburgh P, 1997.

———. "Rhetoric in the Modern University: The Creation of an Underclass." Bullock and Trimbur, pp. 55–84.

Cooper, Marilyn M. "The Ecology of Writing." *College English,* vol. 48, no. 4, 1986, pp. 364–75, doi: 10.2307/377264.

Cronin, Blaise. "Collaboration in Art and in Science: Approaches to Attribution, Authorship, and Acknowledgement." *Information and Culture,* vol. 47, no. 1, 2012, pp. 18–37.

———. "Let the Credits Roll: A Preliminary Examination of the Role Played by Mentors and Trusted Assessors in Disciplinary Formation." *Journal of Documentation,* vol. 47, no. 3, 1991, pp. 227–39, doi: 10.1108/eb026878.

———. *The Scholar's Courtesy: The Role of Acknowledgement in the Primary Communication Process.* Taylor Graham, 1995.

———, Gail McKenzie, and Michael Stiffler. "Patterns of Acknowledgement." *Journal of Documentation,* vol. 48, no. 2, 1992, pp. 107–22, doi: 10.1108/eb026893.

———, Gail McKenzie, and Lourdes Rubio. "The Norms of Acknowledgement in Four Humanities and Social Sciences Disciplines." *Journal of Documentation,* vol. 49, no. 1, 1993, pp. 29–43, doi: 10.1108/eb026909.

———, and Kara Overfelt. "The Scholar's Courtesy: A Survey of Acknowledgement Behaviour." *Journal of Documentation,* vol. 50, no. 3, 1994, pp. 165–96, doi: 10.1108/eb026929.

Couture, Barbara. "Writing and Accountability." Dobrin, Rice, Vastola, pp. 21–40.

Cvetkovich, Ann. *An Archive of Feelings: Trauma, Sexuality, and Lesbian Public Cultures.* Duke UP, 2003.

Derrida, Jacques. *Of Grammatology.* Translated by Gayatri Chakravorty Spivak, Johns Hopkins UP, 1976.

Dobrin, Sidney I., J.A. Rice, and Michael Vastola, editors. *Beyond Postprocess.* Utah SUP, 2011.

Dobrin, Sidney I., and Christian R. Weisser. *Natural Discourse: Toward Ecocomposition.* SUNY P, 2002.

Dolmage, Jay Timothy. *Disability Rhetoric.* Syracuse UP, 2014.

Donahue, Patricia, and Gretchen Flesher Moon, editors. *Local Histories: Reading the Archives of Composition.* U of Pittsburgh P, 2007.

Dunbar-Odom, Donna. *Defying the Odds: Class and the Pursuit of Higher Literacy.* SUNY P, 2006.

Dunn, Patricia A. *Talking, Sketching, Moving: Multiple Literacies in the Teaching of Writing.* Boynton/Cook, 2001.

Ede, Lisa. *Situating Composition: Composition Studies and the Politics of Location.* Southern Illinois UP, 2004.

————, and Andrea A. Lunsford. "Collaboration and Concepts of Authorship." *Writing Together: Collaboration in Theory and Practice*, Bedford/St. Martin's, 2012, pp. 167–85.

Ehrenreich, Barbara. *Bright-Sided: How Positive Thinking is Undermining America.* Picador, 2010.

Elbow, Peter. "Reflections on Academic Discourse: How it Relates to Freshmen and Colleagues." *College English*, vol. 53, no. 2, 1991, pp. 135–55.

Emig, Janet. *The Composing Processes of Twelfth Graders.* National Council of Teachers of English, 1971.

————. "Hand, Eye, Brain: Some 'Basics' in the Writing Process." Emig, *Web*, pp. 110–21.

————. "The Uses of the Unconscious in Composing." Emig, *Web*, pp. 46–53.

————. *The Web of Meaning: Essays on Writing, Teaching, Learning, and Thinking.* Boynton/Cook, 1983.

Epstein, Joseph. "Dedications and Acknowledgements." *Publishers Weekly*, vol. 224, 1983, pp. 43–45.

Faigley, Lester. *Fragments of Rationality: Postmodernity and the Subject of Composition.* U of Pittsburgh P, 1992.

Feldman, Ann M. *Making Writing Matter: Composition in the Engaged University.* SUNY P, 2008.

Flaherty, Alice W. *The Midnight Disease: The Drive to Write, Writer's Block, and the Creative Brain.* Houghton Mifflin, 2004.

"Floating Judgment Box." *Funny Junk*, 25 Nov. 2014, www.funnyjunk.com/Floating +judgment+box/funny-pictures/5367004/.

Foer, Jonathan Safran. "Foreword." Gross and Vallely, pp. ix-xi.

Fowler, Alastair. *How to Write.* Oxford, 2007.

Freedman, Diane P., and Martha Stoddard Holmes, editors. *The Teacher's Body: Embodiment, Authority, and Identity in the Academy.* SUNY P, 2003.

Freire, Paulo. *Pedagogy of the Oppressed.* Translated by Myra Bergman Ramos, 1970, Continuum, 1992.

Gere, Anne Ruggles. *Writing Groups: History, Theory, and Implications.* Southern Illinois UP, 1987.

Giannoni, Davide Simone. "Worlds of Gratitude: A Contrastive Study of Acknowledgment Texts in English and Italian Research Articles." *Applied Linguistics*, vol. 23, no. 1, 2002, pp. 1–31.

Gibson, Michelle. "Revising a (Writer's) Life: Writing with Disability." *Composition Studies*, vol. 41, no. 2, Fall 2013, pp. 12–14, connection.ebscohost.com/c/articles /92549451/revising-a-writers-life-writing-disability.

Goleman, Judith. *Working Theory: Critical Composition Studies for Students and Teachers.* Bergin & Garvey, 1995.

Golpour Lasaki, Farhad. "A Contrastive Study of Generic Organization of Doctoral Dissertation Acknowledgements Written by Native and Non-Native (Iranian) Studies in Applied Linguistics." *Modern Journal of Applied Linguistics: An International Journal*, vol. 3, no. 2, 2011, pp. 175–99.

Golub, Jeffrey. *More Ways to Handle the Paper Load: On Paper and Online*. National Council of Teachers of English, 2005.

Goodman, Paul. *The Break-Up of Our Camp*. New Directions, 1949.

Grafton, Anthony. *The Footnote: A Curious History*. Harvard UP, 1997.

"Gratitude that Grates." *The Economist*, 340, 7 Sept. 1996, pp. 83.

Gross, Aaron. "Introduction and Overview: Animal Others and Animal Studies." Gross and Vallely, pp. 1–23.

Gross, Aaron, and Anne Vallely, editors. *Animals and the Human Imagination: A Companion to Animal Studies*. Columbia UP, 2012.

Gutiérrez y Muhs, Gabriella, Yolanda Flores Niemann, Carmen G. González, and Angela P. Harris, editors. *Presumed Incompetent: The Intersections of Race and Class for Women in Academia*. Utah State UP, 2012.

Haas, Christina. *Writing Technology: Studies on the Materiality of Literacy*. Lawrence Erlbaum, 1996.

Haglund, David. "Stop Hating on Acknowledgments." *Slate*, 3 March 2013, www .slate.com/blogs/browbeat/2013/03/08/acknowledgments_in_books_have_gotten _long_and_sometimes_embarrassing_this.html.

Hamilton, John Maxwell. "The Mistakes in This Essay Are My Own." *New York Times*, 15 Apr 1990: BR1.

Hansen, Kristine, and Christine R. Farris, editors. *College Credit for Writing in High School: The 'Taking Care of' Business*. National Council of Teachers of English, 2010.

Haraway, Donna J. *The Companion Species Manifesto: Dogs, People, and Significant Otherness*. Prickly Paradigm P, 2003.

———. *When Species Meet*. U of Minnesota P, 2007.

Harker, Michael. *The Lure of Literacy: A Critical Reception of the Compulsory Composition Debate*. SUNY P, 2015.

Harris, Joseph. *Rewriting: How to Do Things With Words*. Utah State UP, 2006.

———. *A Teaching Subject: Composition Since 1966*. 2nd ed., Utah State UP, 2012.

Harris, Joseph, John D. Miles, and Charles Paine, editors. *Teaching with Student Texts: Essays Toward an Informed Practice*. Utah State UP, 2010.

Hawhee, Debra. *Moving Bodies: Kenneth Burke at the Edges of Language*. U of South Carolina P, 2009.

Hayles, N. Katherine. *Writing Machines*. MIT P, 2002.

Heilbrun, Margaret. "Best Acknowledgments of 2011." *Library Journal*, 21 Nov. 2011, reviews.libraryjournal.com/2011/11/in-the-bookroom/best-acknowledgments -of-2011/.

———. "Best Acknowledgments of 2012." *Library Journal*. 23 Jan. 2013, reviews .libraryjournal.com/2013/01/in-the-bookroom/authors/best-acknowledgments-of -2012/.

Hesse, Douglas. "Writing and Time, Time and the Essay." *Journal for Expanded Perspectives on Learning*, vol. 18, no. 1, 2012–2013, pp. 1–10, trace.tennessee.edu/jaepl/vol18/iss1/3/.

Hillocks, George, Jr. *Teaching Writing as Reflective Practice*. Teacher's College, 1995.

Hjortshoj, Keith. *Understanding Writing Blocks*. Oxford UP, 2001.

Hoffman, Eva. *Time*. Picador, 2009.

Horner, Bruce, Min-Zhan Lu, and Paul Kei Matsuda. *Cross-Language Relations in Composition*. Southern Illinois UP, 2010.

Horner, Bruce, Min-Zhan Lu, Jacqueline Jones Royster, and John Trimbur. "Opinion: Language Difference in Writing: Toward a Translingual Approach." *College English*, vol. 73, no. 3, 2011, pp. 303–21.

Hyland, Ken. *Disciplinary Discourses: Social Interactions in Academic Writing*. Longman, 2000.

———. "Dissertation Acknowledgements: The Anatomy of a Cinderella Genre." *Written Communication*, vol. 20, no. 3, 2003, pp. 242–68, doi: 10.1177/0741088303257276.

"In the Company of Animals: Emma Straub on Cats and Writing." *The Morgan Library and Museum*, www.themorgan.org/videos/company-animals-emma-straub-cats-and-writing. Accessed 10 June 2015.

"Influence, n." *OED Online*, Oxford University Press, June 2015, www.oed.com/view/Entry/95519?rskey=isbESv&result=1&isAdvanced=false#eid.

Ingold, Tim. *Being Alive: Essays on Movement, Knowledge and Description*. Routledge, 2011.

———. "Hunting and Gathering as Ways of Perceiving the Environment." Gross and Vallely, pp. 31–54.

Irmscher, William F. *Teaching Expository Writing*. 1979. Holt, Rinehart, and Winston, 1987.

Jago, Carol. *Papers, Papers, Papers: An English Teacher's Survival Guide*. Boynton/Cook, 2005.

Jarratt, Susan C., and Lynn Worsham, editors. *Feminism and Composition Studies: In Other Words*. Modern Language Association, 1998.

Johnson-Eilola, Johndan. "Writing about Writing." *Kairos*, vol. 7, no. 3, 2002, kairos.technorhetoric.net/7.3/features/johnsoneilola.htm.

Kassirer, Jerome P., and Marcia Angell. "On Authorship and Acknowledgements." *The New England Journal of Medicine*, vol. 325, no. 21, 21 Nov. 1991, pp. 1510–12.

Kirsch, Gesa E., and Liz Rohan, editors. *Beyond the Archives: Research as a Lived Process*. Southern Illinois UP, 2008.

Kliff, Sarah. "Want to Increase Your Productivity? Study Says: Look at This Adorable Kitten." *The Washington Post*, 1 Oct. 2012, www.washingtonpost.com/blogs/wonkblog/wp/2012/10/01/want-to-increase-your-productivity-study-says-look-at-this-adorable-kitten/.

Knappett, Carl. *Thinking Through Material Culture*. U of Pennsylvania P, 2005.

Knausgaard, Karl Ove. *My Struggle. Book 2: A Man in Love*. Translated by Don Bartlett. Farrar, Straus and Giroux, 2013.

Knoblauch, C. H. "How I Write: An Improbable Fiction." Waldrep, pp. 133–45.

Kroll, Barry M. *The Open Hand: Arguing as an Art of Peace*. Utah State UP, 2013.

Kubrick, Stanley, director. *The Shining*. Warner Brothers, 1980.

Latour, Bruno. "Agency at the Time of the Anthropocene." *New Literary History*, vol. 45, no. 1, Winter 2014, pp. 1–18, doi: 10.1353/nlh.2014.0003.

Lauer, Janice M. *Invention in Rhetoric and Composition*. Parlor Press and WAC Clearinghouse, 2004, https://wac.colostate.edu/books/lauer_invention/.

Leon, Kendall, and Stacey Pigg. "Graduate Students Professionalizing in Digital Time/ Space: A View from 'Down Below.'" *Computers and Composition*, vol. 28, no. 1, 2011, pp. 3–13, dx.doi.org/10.1016/j.compcom.2010.12.002.

Lewiecki-Wilson, and Brenda Jo Brueggemann, editors. *Disability and the Teaching of Writing: A Critical Sourcebook*. Bedford/St. Martin's, 2008.

Lindemann, Erika. *A Rhetoric for Writing Teachers*. 3rd ed. Oxford UP, 1995.

Lloyd-Jones, Richard. "Playing for Mortal Stakes." Waldrep, pp. 153–63.

Lorch, Sue. "Confessions of a Former Sailor." Waldrep, pp. 165–71.

Luke, Carmen, editor. *Feminisms and Pedagogies of Everyday Life*. SUNY P, 1996.

Lunsford, Andrea, and Lisa Ede. "Why Write . . . Together: A Research Update." *Rhetoric Review*, vol. 5, no. 1, 1986, pp. 71–81, www.jstor.org/stable/46602.

Lunsford, Richard. "Preface." *Key Works on Teacher Response: An Anthology*, edited by Richard Straub, Boynton/Cook, 2006, pp. xi–xii.

Lynn, Steven. *Rhetoric and Composition: An Introduction*. Cambridge UP, 2010.

Macintosh, K.H. *Acknowledgement Patterns in Sociology*. Dissertation, University of Oregon, 1972. UMI, 1972.

Malone, Noreen. "Thank You to the Author's Many, Many Important Friends: How the Acknowledgments Page Became the Place to Drop Names." *New Republic*, 7 March 2013, www.newrepublic.com/article/112578/what-sheryl-sandbergs -acknowledgments-reveals#.

McCain, Katherine W. "Communication, Competition, and Secrecy: The Production and Dissemination of Research-Related Information in Genetics." *Science, Technology, & Human Values*, vol. 16, no. 4, 1991, pp. 491–516, doi: 10.1177/016224399101600404.

McCracken, Nancy Mellin, and Bruce C. Appleby, editors. *Gender Issues in the Teaching of English*. Boynton/Cook, 1992.

McDonald, Christina Russell, and Robert L. McDonald, editors. *Teaching Writing: Landmarks and Horizons*. Southern Illinois UP, 2002.

McKenna, Erin. "Pets in the Academic Workplace." *Times Higher Education*, 28 Nov. 2013, www.timeshighereducation.co.uk/comment/opinion/pets-in-the-academic -workplace/2009308.article.

McQuerrey, Lisa. "Why Taking Pets to Work Enhances Productivity & Improves Mood." Chron, smallbusiness.chron.com/taking-pets-work-enhances-productivity -improves-mood-74806.html. Accessed 6 Aug. 2015.

Micciche, Laura R. *The Cultural Work of Composition Studies: Differencing Knowledge in the Age of Professionalization*. Dissertation, University of Wisconsin-Milwaukee, 1999. UMI, 1999.

———. *Doing Emotion: Rhetoric, Writing, Teaching*. Boynton/Cook, 2007.

———. "For Slow Agency." *Writing Program Administration*, vol. 35, no. 1, Fall/Winter 2011, pp. 73–90, wpacouncil.org/archives/35n1/35n1micciche.pdf.

Milic, Louis T. "How a Stylistician Writes." Waldrep, pp. 199–213.

Miller, Caroline R. "Genre as Social Action." *Quarterly Journal of Speech*, vol. 70, no. 2, 1984, pp. 151–67, doi: 10.1080/00335638409383686.

Miller, J. Hillis. "The Critic as Host." *Critical Inquiry*, vol, 3, no. 3, 1977, pp. 439–47, www.jstor.org/stable/1342933.

Miller, Susan. "Rebelling Against the All." *Writers on Writing, Volume II*, edited by Tom Waldrep, Random House, 1985, pp. 167–75.

———. *Textual Carnivals: The Politics of Composition*. Southern Illinois UP, 1993.

Mingwei, Zhao, and Jiang Yajun. "Dissertation Acknowledgments: Generic Structure and Linguistic Features." *Chinese Journal of Applied Linguistics*, vol. 33, no. 1, 2010, pp. 94–109, connection.ebscohost.com/c/articles/57233899/dissertation-acknowledgments-generic-structure-linguistic-features.

Minkel, Elizabeth. "Writing with Cats." *The New Yorker*, 21 April 2011, www.newyorker.com/books/page-turner/writing-with-cats.

Mohammadi, Mohammad Javad. "Do Persian and English Dissertation Acknowledgments Accommodate Hyland's Model: A Cross-Linguistic Study." *International Journal of Academic Research in Business and Social Sciences*, vol. 3, no. 5, 2013, pp. 534–47.

Monroe, Barbara. *Plateau Indian Ways with Words: The Rhetorical Tradition of the Tribes of the Inland Pacific Northwest*. U of Pittsburgh P, 2014.

Mortensen, Peter. "Reading Material." *Written Communication*, vol. 18, no. 4, 2001, pp. 395–439.

Murakami, Haruki. "The Art of Fiction No. 182." *The Paris Review*, no. 170, 2004, www.theparisreview.org/interviews/2/the-art-of-fiction-no-182-haruki-murakami.

———. *What I Talk About When I Talk About Running*. Translated by Philip Gabriel, Vintage, 2008.

The National Commission on Excellence in Education. *A Nation at Risk: The Imperative for Educational Reform*. United States Department of Education, 1983.

Nicotra, Jodie. "'Folksonomy' and the Restructuring of Writing Space." *College Composition and Communication*, vol. 61, no. 1, 2009, W259-76, www.ncte.org/library/nctefiles/resources/journals/ccc/0611-sep09/ccc0611folks.pdf.

Olson, Gary A., and Lynn Worsham, editors. *Critical Intellectuals on Writing*. SUNY P, 2003.

———. "Slavoj Žižek" pp. 192–200.

Owens, Erica. "Significant Others." *Blackwell Encyclopedia of Sociology*, Blackwell Reference Online, 4 Aug. 2015, doi: 10.1111/b.9781405124331.2007.x.

Payne, Michelle. *Bodily Discourses: When Students Write About Abuse and Eating Disorders*. Boynton/Cook, 2000.

Peng, Hua. *Chinese PhD Thesis Acknowledgements: A Communities of Practice Perspective*. Peter Lang, 2010.

Perelman, Les. "Construct Validity, Length, Score, and Time in Holistically Graded Writing Assessments: The Case Against Automated Essay Scoring." *International Advances in Writing Research: Cultures, Places, Measures*, edited by Charles Bazerman, Chris Dean, Jessica Early, Karen Lunsford, Suzie Null, Paul Rogers, and Amanda Stansell. WAC Clearinghouse, Parlor, P, 2012, pp. 121–32, wac.colostate.edu/books/wrab2011/.

Perl, Sondra. *Felt Sense: Writing with the Body*. Boynton/Cook, 2004.

————. "Understanding Composing." *College Composition and Communication*, vol. 31, no. 4, 1980, pp. 363–69, doi: 10.2307/356586.

Phelps, Louise Wetherbee. *Composition as a Human Science: Contributions to the Self-Understanding of a Discipline*. Oxford UP, 1988.

————. "Rhythm and Pattern in a Composing Life." Waldrep, pp. 241–57.

Pickering, Andrew. "Being in an Environment: A Performative Perspective." *Natures Sciences Sociétés*, vol. 21, no. 1, 2013, pp. 77–83, doi: 10.1051/nss/2013067.

Popova, Maria. "Fiona Apple's Defense of Canceling Concerts to be With Her Dying Dog." *The Atlantic*, 26 Nov. 2012, www.theatlantic.com/health/archive/2012/11/fiona-apples-defense-of-canceling-concerts-to-be-with-her-dying-dog/265573/.

Potter, Claire. "Giving Thanks: An Essay on Acknowledgments." *The Chronicle*, 22 Nov. 2006, chronicle.com/blognetwork/tenuredradical/2006/11/giving-thanks-grumpy-essay-on/.

Prendergast, Catherine, and Roman Ličko. "The Ethos of Paper: Here and There." *jac*, vol. 29, no. 1–2, 2009, pp. 199–28, www.jstor.org/stable/20866891.

Price, Margaret. *Mad at School: Rhetorics of Mental Disability and Academic Life*. U of Michigan P, 2011.

Prior, Paul. *Writing/Disciplinarity: A Sociohistoric Account of Literate Activity in the Academy*. L. Erlbaum Associates, 1998.

Prior, Paul, and Jody Shipka. "Chronotopic Lamination: Tracing the Contours of Literate Activity." *Writing Selves/Writing Societies: Research from Activity Perspectives*, edited by Charles Bazerman and David R. Russell. WAC Clearinghouse, 2003, pp. 180–238.

Probyn, Elspeth. "Writing Shame." Gregg and Seigworth, pp. 71–90.

Qualley, Donna. *Turns of Thought: Teaching Composition as Reflexive Inquiry*. Boynton/Cook, 1997.

Ratcliffe, Krista. *Rhetorical Listening: Identification, Gender, Whiteness*. Southern Illinois UP, 2005.

Reynolds, Nedra. *Geographies of Writing: Inhabiting Places and Encountering Difference*. Southern Illinois UP, 2004.

Rich, Adrienne. *Of Woman Born: Motherhood as Experience and Institution*. 10th Anniversary ed. W. W. Norton and Company, 1986.

Rickert, Thomas. *Ambient Rhetoric: The Attunements of Rhetorical Being*. U of Pittsburgh P, 2013.

Ridolfo, Jim, and Dànielle Nicole Devoss. "Composing for Recomposition: Rhetorical Velocity and Delivery." *Kairos*, vol. 13, no. 2, 15 Jan. 2009, kairos.technorhetoric.net/13.2/topoi/ridolfo_devoss/intro.html.

Robinson, Andrew. *The Story of Writing*. 2nd ed. Thames & Hudson, 2007.

Rose, Mike, editor. *When a Writer Can't Write*. Guilford, 1985.

Royster, Jacqueline Jones, and Gesa E. Kirsch. *Feminist Rhetorical Practices: New Horizons for Rhetoric, Composition, and Literacy Studies*. Southern Illinois UP, 2012.

Sacks, Sam. "Against Acknowledgments." *The New Yorker*, 24 Aug. 2012, www.newyorker.com/online/blogs/books/2012/08/against-acknowledgments.html#ixzz2MyMS5tHo.

Sánchez, Raúl. *The Function of Theory in Composition Studies.* SUNY P, 2005.

Sandberg, Sheryl. *Lean In: Women, Work, and the Will to Lead.* Knopf, 2013.

Schell, Eileen E, and Patricia Lambert Stock. *Moving a Mountain: Transforming the Role of Contingent Faculty in Composition Studies and Higher Education.* National Council of Teachers of English, 2001.

Schilb, John. *Between the Lines: Relating Composition Theory and Literary Theory.* Heinemann, 1996.

Scholes, Robert. *The Rise and Fall of English: Reconstructing English as a Discipline.* Yale UP, 1998.

Serpell, James. *In the Company of Animals: A Study of Human-Animal Relationships.* Cambridge UP, 1996.

Shaughnessy, Mina P. *Errors and Expectations: A Guide for the Teacher of Basic Writing.* Oxford UP, 1977.

Shipka, Jody. *Toward a Composition Made Whole.* U of Pittsburgh P, 2011.

Shor, Ira. *Critical Teaching and Everyday Life.* 1980. U of Chicago P, 1987.

Sicha, Choire. "The Name-Drop Acknowledgement and the Unrestrained Gushing of Privilege." *The Awl,* 7 March 2013. www.theawl.com/2013/03/the-name-drop-acknowledgement-and-the-unrestrained-gushing-of-privilege.

Slick, Joseph. *Emotional Literacy and the Challenge of ESL Academic Literacy.* Dissertation, Indiana University of Pennsylvania, 2012. UMI, 2012.

Sommers, Nancy. "Revision Strategies of Student Writers and Experienced Adult Writers." *College Composition and Communication,* vol. 31, no. 4, Dec. 1980, pp. 378–88, doi: 10.2307/356588.

Sontag, Susan. "On Paul Goodman." *Under the Sign of Saturn,* Farrar, Straus, Giroux, 1980, pp. 3–10.

Stenberg, Shari J. *Professing and Pedagogy: Learning the Teaching of English.* National Council of Teachers of English, 2005.

Stewart, Kathleen. *Ordinary Affects.* Duke UP, 2007.

Strausser, Jeffrey. *Painless Writing.* 2nd ed. Barron's Educational Series, 2009.

Strickland, Donna. "Beyond Belief: Embodiment and the 'Trying Game.'" *Journal for Expanded Perspectives on Learning,* vol. 15, winter 2009–2010, pp. 78–86, trace.tennessee.edu/cgi/viewcontent.cgi?article=1170&context=jaepl.

———. *The Managerial Unconscious in the History of Composition Studies.* Southern Illinois UP, 2011.

"Student Veterans in the College Composition Classroom: Realizing Their Strengths and Assessing Their Needs." *National Council of Teachers of English,* March 2015. www.ncte.org/cccc/resources/positions/student-veterans.

Sullivan, Harry Stack. *Conceptions of Modern Psychiatry.* Norton, 1947.

———. *The Interpersonal Theory of Psychiatry.* Norton, 1953.

Syverson, Margaret A. *The Wealth of Reality: An Ecology of Composition.* Southern Illinois UP, 1999.

Tassoni, John Paul, and William H. Thelin, editors. *Blundering for a Change: Errors and Expectations in Critical Pedagogy.* Boynton/Cook, 2000.

Tomlinson, Barbara. *Authors on Writing: Metaphors and Intellectual Labor.* Palgrave, 2005.

Tomlinson, John. *The Culture of Speed: The Coming of Immediacy*. Sage, 2007.

Trimbur, John. "Composition and the Circulation of Writing." *College Composition and Communication*, vol. 52, no. 2, 2000, pp. 188–219.

———, and Karen Press. "The Page as a Unit of Discourse: Notes toward a Counterhistory for Writing Studies." Dobrin et al., pp. 94–113.

Turkle, Sherry, editor. *Evocative Objects: Things We Think With*. MIT P, 2007.

"University of Chicago Press Manuscript Preparation Guidelines." *The University of Chicago Press*, 19 March 2013. www.press.uchicago.edu/infoServices/emsguide.html.

Van Etten, Sharon. *Tramp*. Jagjaguwar, 2012.

Villanueva, Victor. *Bootstraps: From an American Academic of Color*. National Council of Teachers of English, 1993.

Vitanza, Victor J., editor. *Writing Histories of Rhetoric*. Southern Illinois UP, 1994.

Waldrep, Tom, editor. *Writers on Writing*. Random House, 1985.

———. *Writers on Writing*. Vol. 2, Random House, 1987.

Walvoord, Barbara E. Fassler. *Helping Students Write Well: A Guide for Teachers in All Disciplines*. 2nd ed, Modern Language Association, 1986.

Wardle, Elizabeth, and Douglas Downs. "Teaching about Writing, Righting Misconceptions: (Re)Envisioning 'First-Year Composition' as 'Introduction to Writing Studies.'" *College Composition and Communication*, vol. 58, no. 4, 2007, pp. 552–84.

Warnock, Tilly. "How I Write." Waldrep, pp. 305–15.

Weaver, Constance. *Teaching Grammar in Context*. Boynton/Cook, 1996.

"Welcome." *OmmWriter*, 7 July 2015, www.ommwriter.com/.

White, Edward. "An Apologia for the Timed Impromptu Essay Test." *College Composition and Communication*, vol. 46, no. 1, 1995, pp. 30–45, doi: 10.2307/358868.

Williams, Joseph M. *Style: Ten Lessons in Clarity and Grace*. 3rd ed, HarperCollins, 1989.

Williams, Raymond. "The Tenses of the Imagination." *Tenses of Imagination: Raymond Williams on Science Fiction, Utopia and Dystopia*, edited by Andrew Milner, Peter Lang, 2010, pp. 113–26.

Wilson, James C., and Cynthia Lewiecki-Wilson. "Constructing a Third Space: Disability Studies, the Teaching of English, and Institutional Transformation." *Disability Studies: Enabling the Humanities*, edited by Sharon L. Snyder, Brenda Jo Brueggemann, and Rosemarie Garland-Thomson, Modern Language Association, 2002, pp. 296–307.

Winterowd, W. Ross. "The Composing Process Paper." Waldrep, pp. 329–41.

Woelfel, Joseph, and Archibald O. Haller. "Significant Others, the Self-Reflexive Act and the Attitude Formation Process." *American Sociological Review*, vol. 36, no. 1, Feb. 1971, pp. 74–87, www.jstor.org/stable/2093508.

Woodworth, Marc, and Ally-Jane Grossman, editors. *How to Write About Music: Excerpts from the 331/3 Series, Magazines, Books and Blogs with Advice from Industry-leading Writers*. Bloomsbury, 2015.

Yagoda, Ben. *How to Not Write Bad: The Most Common Writing Problems and the Best Ways to Avoid Them*. Riverhead Trade, 2013.

Works Cited

Young, Vershawn Ashanti, Rusty Barrett, Y'Shanda Young-Rivera, and Kim Brian Lovejoy. *Code-Meshing, Code-Switching, and African American Literacy*. Teachers College Press, 2013.

APPENDICES

APPENDIX A: ACKNOWLEDGMENTS REFERENCED

Full bibliographic information can be found in the list of works cited. Many more books were consulted than are found in this list.

1. Linda Adler-Kassner, *The Activist WPA: Changing Stories about Writing and Writers* (2008)
2. Sara Ahmed, *On Being Included: Racism and Diversity in Institutional Life* (2012)
3. Adam J. Banks, *Race, Rhetoric, and Technology: Searching for Higher Ground* (2006)
4. Anis Bawarshi, *Genre and the Invention of the Writer: Reconsidering the Place of Invention in Composition* (2003)
5. Pat Belanoff and Marcia Dickson, *Portfolios: Process and Product* (1991)
6. Sarah Benesch, *Considering Emotions in Critical English Language Teaching: Theories and Praxis* (2012)
7. Jane Bennett, *Vibrant Matter: A Political Ecology of Things* (2010)
8. Jeffrey Berman, *Empathic Teaching: Education for Life* (2004)
9. Ann E. Berthoff and James Stephens, *Forming/Thinking/Writing* (1988)
10. Lynn Z. Bloom, *Composition Studies as a Creative Art: Teaching, Writing, Scholarship, Administration* (1998)
11. Megan Boler, *Feeling Power: Emotions and Education* (1999)
12. Lee-Ann Kastman Breuch, *Virtual Peer Review: Teaching and Learning about Writing in Online Environments* (2004)
13. Linda Brodkey, *Writing Permitted in Designated Areas Only* (1996)
14. Miriam Brody, *Manly Writing: Gender, Rhetoric, and the Rise of Composition* (1993)
15. Lizbeth Bryant, *Voice as Process* (2005)
16. A. Suresh Canagarajah, *A Geopolitics of Academic Writing* (2002)
17. Colin Charlton, Jonikka Charlton, Tarez Samra Graban, Kathleen J. Ryan, and Amy Ferdinandt Stolley, *GenAdmin: Theorizing WPA Identities in the Twenty-First Century* (2011)
18. Andy Clark, *Being There: Putting Brain, Body, and World Together Again* (1997)
19. Robert J. Connors, *Composition-Rhetoric: Backgrounds, Theory, and Pedagogy* (1997)

20. Ann Cvetkovich, *An Archive of Feelings: Trauma, Sexuality, and Lesbian Public Cultures* (2003)

21. D. Diane Davis, *Inessential Solidarity: Rhetoric and Foreigner Relations* (2010)

22. Sidney I. Dobrin and Christian R. Weisser, *Natural Discourse: Toward Ecocomposition* (2002)

23. Patricia Donahue and Gretchen Flesher Moon, editors, *Local Histories: Reading the Archives of Composition* (2007)

24. Donna Dunbar-Odom, *Defying the Odds: Class and the Pursuit of Higher Literacy* (2006)

25. Lisa Ede, *Situating Composition: Composition Studies and the Politics of Location* (2004)

26. Ann M. Feldman, *Making Writing Matter: Composition in the Engaged University* (2008)

27. Diane P. Freedman and Martha Stoddard Holmes, eds., *The Teacher's Body: Embodiment, Authority, and Identity in the Academy* (2003)

28. Judith Goleman, *Working Theory: Critical Composition Studies for Students and Teachers* (1995)

29. Christina Haas, *Writing Technology: Studies on the Materiality of Literacy* (1996)

30. Donna Haraway, *When Species Meet* (2007)

31. Joseph Harris, *Rewriting: How to Do Things With Words* (2006)

32. Joseph Harris, *A Teaching Subject: Composition Since 1966* (2012)

33. Joseph Harris, John D. Miles, Charles Paine, eds., *Teaching with Student Texts: Essays Toward an Informed Practice* (2010)

34. Debra Hawhee, *Moving Bodies: Kenneth Burke at the Edges of Language* (2009)

35. N. Katherine Hayles, *Writing Machines* (2002)

36. George Hillocks Jr., *Teaching Writing as Reflective Practice* (1995)

37. Tim Ingold, *Being Alive: Essays on Movement, Knowledge and Description* (2011)

38. William F. Irmscher, *Teaching Expository Writing* (1987)

39. Susan C. Jarratt and Lynn Worsham, *Feminism and Composition Studies: In Other Words* (1998)

40. Gesa E. Kirsch and Liz Rohan, eds., *Beyond the Archives: Research as a Lived Process* (2008)

41. Carl Knappett, *Thinking Through Material Culture* (2005)

42. Janice M. Lauer, *Invention in Rhetoric and Composition* (2004)

43. Erika Lindemann, *A Rhetoric for Writing Teachers*, 3rd ed. (1995)

44. Carmen Luke, ed., *Feminisms and Pedagogies of Everyday Life* (1996)

45. Richard Lunsford, *Key Works on Teacher Response: An Anthology* (Richard Straub, ed.) (2006)

46. Steven Lynn, *Rhetoric and Composition: An Introduction* (2010)

47. Nancy Mellin McCracken and Bruce C. Appleby, eds., *Gender Issues in the Teaching of English* (1992)

48. Christina Russell McDonald and Robert L. McDonald, eds., *Teaching Writing: Landmarks and Horizons* (2002)

49. Laura R. Micciche, *The Cultural Work of Composition Studies: Differencing Knowledge in the Age of Professionalization* (1999)

50. Laura R. Micciche, *Doing Emotion: Rhetoric, Writing, Teaching* (2007)

51. Barbara Monroe, *Plateau Indian Ways with Words: The Rhetorical Tradition of the Tribes of the Tribes of the Inland Pacific Northwest* (2014)

52. Michelle Payne, *Bodily Discourses: When Students Write About Abuse and Eating Disorders* (2000)

53. Sondra Perl, *Felt Sense: Writing with the Body* (2004)

54. Louise Wetherbee Phelps, *Composition as a Human Science: Contributions to the Self-Understanding of a Discipline* (1988)

55. Margaret Price, *Mad at School: Rhetorics of Mental Disability and Academic Life* (2011)

56. Paul Prior, *Writing/Disciplinarity: A Sociohistoric Account of Literate Activity in the Academy* (2003)

57. Donna Qualley, *Turns of Thought: Teaching Composition as Reflexive Inquiry* (1997)

58. Krista Ratcliffe, *Rhetorical Listening: Identification, Gender, Whiteness* (2005)

59. Nedra Reynolds, *Geographies of Writing: Inhabiting Places and Encountering Difference* (2004)

60. Thomas Rickert, *Ambient Rhetoric: The Attunements of Rhetorical Being* (2013)

61. Mike Rose, ed., *When a Writer Can't Write* (1985)

62. Jacqueline Jones Royster and Gesa E. Kirsch, eds., *Feminist Rhetorical Practices: New Horizons for Rhetoric, Composition, and Literacy Studies* (2012)

63. Raúl Sánchez, *The Function of Theory in Composition Studies* (2005)

64. Eileen E. Schell and Patricia Lambert Stock, eds., *Moving a Mountain: Transforming the Role of Contingent Faculty in Composition Studies and Higher Education* (2001)

65. Robert Scholes, *The Rise and Fall of English: Reconstructing English as a Discipline* (1998)

66. Mina P. Shaughnessy, *Errors and Expectations: A Guide for the Teacher of Basic Writing* (1977)
67. Jody Shipka, *Toward a Composition Made Whole* (2011)
68. Ira Shor, *Critical Teaching and Everyday Life* (1987)
69. Joseph Slick, *Emotional Literacy and the Challenge of ESL Academic Literacy* (2012)
70. Shari J. Stenberg, *Professing and Pedagogy: Learning the Teaching of English* (2005)
71. Kathleen Stewart, *Ordinary Affects* (2007)
72. Donna Strickland, *The Managerial Unconscious in the History of Composition Studies* (2011)
73. Margaret A. Syverson, *The Wealth of Reality: An Ecology of Composition* (1999)
74. John Paul Tassoni and William H. Thelin, eds., *Blundering for a Change: Errors and Expectations in Critical Pedagogy* (2000)
75. Sharon Van Etten, *Tramp* (2012)
76. Victor Villanueva, *Bootstraps: From an American Academic of Color* (1993)
77. Victor J. Vitanza, ed., *Writing Histories of Rhetoric* (1994)
78. Constance Weaver, *Teaching Grammar in Context* (1996)
79. Joseph M. Williams, *Style: Ten Lessons in Clarity and Grace* (1989)

APPENDIX B: SURVEY AND IRB
APPROVAL DOCUMENTATION

Institutional Review Board - Federalwide Assurance #00003152

University of Cincinnati

Date: 2/14/2014

From: UC IRB

To: Principal Investigator: Laura Micciche
A&S English & Comparative Literature

Re: Study ID: 2013-6520
Study Title: Acknowledging Writing Partners

The above referenced protocol and all applicable additional documentation provided to the IRB were reviewed and **APPROVED** using an **EXPEDITED** review procedure in accordance with 45 CFR 46.110(b) (1)(see below) on **2/14/2014**.

This study will be due for continuing review at least 30 days before: 2/13/2015.

Study Documents

Attachment A Recruitment email.doc

Attachment B Information Sheet.doc

Conflict of Interest.doc

CV_scribd_10-13.pdf

Protocol+Template+-+SBR+6-11-09.doc

Survey.pdf

Please note the following requirements:

Consent Requirements
Per 45 CFR 46.117 (21 CFR 56.109) the IRB has waived the requirement to obtain DOCUMENTATION of informed consent for all adult participants.

AMENDMENTS: The principal investigator is responsible for notifying the IRB of any changes in the protocol, participating investigators, procedures, recruitment, consent forms, FDA status, or

https://epas.research.cchmc.org/ePAS_PRD/Doc/0/HM172CBLNML47874DUG0LTF36D/fromString.html[2/14/14 3:45:36 PM] conflicts of interest. Approval is based on the information as submitted. New procedures cannot be initiated until IRB approval has been given. If you wish to change any aspect of this study, please submit an Amendment via ePAS to the IRB, providing a justification for each requested change.

CONTINUING REVIEW: The investigator is responsible for submitting a Continuing Review via ePAS to the IRB at least 30 days prior to the expiration date listed above. Please note that study procedures may only continue into the next cycle if the IRB has reviewed and granted re-approval prior to the expiration date.

UNANTICIPATED PROBLEMS: The investigator is responsible for reporting unanticipated problems promptly to the IRB via ePAS according to current reporting policies.

STUDY COMPLETION: The investigator is responsible for notifying the IRB by submitting a Request to Close via ePAS when the research, including data analysis, has completed.

Please note: This approval is through the IRB only. You may be responsible for reporting to other regulatory officials (e.g. VA Research and Development Office, UC Health – University Hospital). Please check with your institution and department to ensure you have met all reporting requirements.

Statement regarding International conference on Harmonization and Good clinical Practices. The Institutional Review Board is duly constituted (fulfilling FDA requirements for diversity), has written procedures for initial and continuing review of clinical trials: prepares written minutes of convened meetings and retains records pertaining to the review and approval process; all in compliance with requirements defined in 21 CFR Parts 50, 56 and 312 Code of Federal Regulations. This institution is in compliance with the ICH GCP as adopted by FDA/DHHS.

Thank you for your cooperation during the review process.

Research Categories

6. Collection of data from voice, video, digital, or image recordings made for research purposes.

---

7. Research on individual or group characteristics or behavior (including, but not limited to, research on perception, cognition, motivation, identity, language, communication, cultural beliefs or practices, and social behavior) or research employing survey, interview, oral history, focus group, program evaluation, human factors evaluation, or quality assurance methodologies. (NOTE: Some research in this category may be exempt from the HHS regulations for the protection of human subjects. 45 CFR 46.101(b)(2) and (b)(3). This listing refers only to research that is not exempt.)

Information Sheet for Research
University of Cincinnati
Department: English
Principal Investigator: Laura Micciche, PhD

Title of Study: Acknowledging Writing Partners

Introduction:
You are being asked to take part in a research study. Please read this paper carefully and ask questions about anything that you do not understand.

Who is doing this research study?
The person in charge of this research study is Laura Micciche, Associate Professor of English at the University of Cincinnati. She is conducting research for a book called Acknowledging Writing Partners, a study of writing's often hidden vitality and materiality as seen through the lens of the genre of acknowledgments. One chapter will focus on the role of animal companions in writing activities.

What is the purpose of this research study?
The purpose of this research study is to study the role of animal companions in writing activities.

Who will be in this research study?
About 25-100 people will take part in this study. Participants may be in this study if they are a) full-time tenured or non-tenured writing faculty or doctoral students in the field of Composition Studies, and b) those who regularly write in spaces shared with animals.

What will you be asked to do in this research study, and how long will it take?
You will be asked to complete an online survey about the role of animals during composing. The survey should take about 10-15 minutes.

In addition to the survey, participants will be invited to submit photos depicting the role of animals in one's writing environment to a private Facebook group.

Finally, participants will be invited to volunteer for a 20-minute follow-up interview via phone or face-to-face that will be audiotaped.

Are there any risks to being in this research study?
There are no risks associated with being in this research study.

Are there any benefits from being in this research study?
There are no individual benefits to participation in the survey, except the opportunity for self-reflection on the importance of animals to one's writing life. This study is expected to benefit the continued evolution of writing theory and practice.

What will you get because of being in this research study?
You will not be paid for your participation.

Do you have choices about taking part in this research study?
If you do not want to answer the survey questions you may simply exit the survey without submitting it. If you complete the survey, you can choose not to do the other activities.

You may choose whether or not to have your name associated with your comments. You may indicate your choice at the end of the survey. If you indicate willingness to be interviewed, all interviews will be audiotaped. If you do not want to be audiotaped you should choose not to participate in the interview part of this study.

How will your research information be kept confidential?
Information you provide on Survey Monkey will not have your name attached, unless you wish to identify yourself. Information submitted through Facebook or during the follow-up interview will be identifiable. The researcher cannot ensure privacy of information sent through Facebook or over the Internet.

Your identifiable information will be kept on the researcher's password-protected computer. The researcher plans retain your data until she has written up findings, revised, and published the resulting study. After that, the researcher will destroy the data.

Agents of the University of Cincinnati may inspect study records for audit or quality assurance purposes.

What are your legal rights in this research study?
Nothing in this consent form waives any legal rights you may have. This consent form also does not release the investigator, the institution, or its

agents from liability for negligence.

What if you have questions about this research study?
If you have any questions or concerns about this research study, you should contact Dr. Laura Micciche, at laura.micciche@uc.edu or 513-556-6519.

The UC Institutional Review Board reviews all research projects that involve human participants to be sure the rights and welfare of participants are protected.

If you have questions about your rights as a participant or complaints about the study, you may contact the UC IRB at (513) 558-5259. Or, you may call the UC Research Compliance Hotline at (800) 889-1547, or write to the IRB, 300 University Hall, ML 0567, 51 Goodman Drive, Cincinnati, OH 45221-0567, or email the IRB office at irb@ucmail.uc.edu.

Do you HAVE to take part in this research study?
No one has to be in this research study. Refusing to take part will NOT cause any penalty or loss of benefits that you would otherwise have. You may start and then change your mind and stop at any time. To stop being in the study, you should tell Dr. Laura Micciche, at laura.micciche@uc.edu or 513-556-6519

SUBMITTING YOUR COMPLETED SURVEY INDICATES YOUR CONSENT FOR YOUR ANSWERS TO BE USED IN THIS RESEARCH STUDY.

At the end of the survey, you will be asked if you would like your name associated with your comments. This is completely optional.

About You

＊1. Do you regularly write in spaces shared with animals?

◯ Yes

◯ No (if this is your reply, please exit this survey)

＊2. Please mark the category below that best describes your status in Composition Studies (or its cognates: Writing Studies; Rhetoric and Composition; Rhetoric, Literacy, & Composition, etc.). If none, please exit the survey.

◯ Full-time faculty member (tenured)

◯ Full-time faculty member (nontenured)

◯ Doctoral Student

Writing Practices

✱3. Identify the kinds of writing that you regularly engage in (select all that apply):

- ☐ Scholarship
- ☐ Teaching materials
- ☐ Administrative documents
- ☐ Editorial correspondence
- ☐ Emails

- ☐ Texts (SMS)
- ☐ Chat exchanges
- ☐ Reviews of scholarship for journals or presses
- ☐ Personal writing
- ☐ Creative writing

- ☐ Letters to friends or family
- ☐ Community-based writing
- ☐ Blog posts
- ☐ Gaming chats

Add forms of writing not mentioned above and/or elaborate on any of the forms you identfied above.

✱4. Identify locations where you generate most of your writing (you may select more than one).

- ☐ Home
- ☐ Office
- ☐ Library

- ☐ Coffee shop
- ☐ Friend's abode
- ☐ Bar

- ☐ Restaurant
- ☐ Outdoors

If you write in locales not mentioned above, please list them here.

✱5. Identify tools you most often use to generate writing (select all that apply).

- ☐ Computer
- ☐ Tablet
- ☐ Phone

- ☐ Paper and pen/pencil
- ☐ Moleskine

Other (please specify)

Animals & Composing

✱6. Identify the animal(s) that are a regular part of the scene of writing for you (select all that apply).

☐ Cat   ☐ Lizard   ☐ Turtle

☐ Dog   ☐ Hamster   ☐ Snake

☐ Rabbit   ☐ Bird

Other (please specify)

✱7. Please identify the number of animals who are a regular part of your writing scene.

○ 1

○ 2

○ 3

○ 4

○ 5

○ 6

Other (please specify)

✱8. Explain what kind of contact you have with animals while writing (select all that apply).

☐ Petting   ☐ Animal near you in the room

☐ Animal sits/rests on you   ☐ Talking to the animal

Other and/or add more detail to the above

＊9. Identify values that animals seem to contribute to your writing process.

☐ Patience   ☐ Endurance   ☐ Comfort

☐ Frustration   ☐ Pleasure   ☐ Stress

☐ Kindness   ☐ Focus   ☐ Relaxation

☐ Worry   ☐ Distraction   ☐ Perspective

Please add values not mentioned above.

＊10. For this study, I am thinking of animals as "writing companions." Reflect upon this phrasing for a moment and then free associate what comes to mind for you. Please also address whether this phrasing resonates with you (and then explain why or why not).

11. Please feel free to add anything relevant to your relationship with animals in scenes of writing that you didn't have the opportunity to say above.

Other Ways to Contribute

12. Please indicate whether or not the researcher may cite your name in association with your comments.

○ NO, I do NOT want my name to be associated with my comments.

○ YES, my name may be associated with my comments.

If you selected "yes," please enter your name here.

13. If you are willing to submit photos of animals in your writing environment to a private Facebook group, please input your email address. I will send you an invitation to the group page.

14. I will select some participants for follow-up interviews to this survey. If you are interested in participating in a 20-minute interview, please add your name and email address below. Depending on preference and availability, interviews will be conducted by phone or face-to-face.

Thank you for your participation! If you have any questions about this survey and/or my research project, please feel free to contact me at laura.micciche@uc.edu or 513-556-6519. I appreciate your time and support!

Laura Micciche

APPENDIX C: PRIVATE FACEBOOK GROUP DESCRIPTION AND INSTRUCTIONS

A place where writers can post photos of animals in their writing environments. Feel free to add comments as well. Only those who completed my online survey, entitled Composing with Animals, and volunteered to submit photos are invited to post on this site.

As a reminder, I am collecting these photos for use in a forthcoming book, tentatively titled "Acknowledging Writing Partners." As such, I will select some photos to reproduce in the completed book; please keep this in mind when posting! Contributors retain copyright of their works and, in accordance with the conditions of the Creative Commons Attribution-Share-Alike license (http://creativecommons.org/licenses/by-sa/3.0/us/), I will give appropriate credit to contributors and indicate if changes are made to a photo.

The group is a "secret" group, so only members see the group, who's in it, and what members post. Thanks for agreeing to participate and supporting my research with your contributions! I look forward to seeing your photos.

Cheers,

Laura Micciche

University of Cincinnati

APPENDIX D: CODING ASSOCIATIONS WITH THE PHRASING "WRITING PARTNERSHIPS"

Note: If a sample appears to be codable in two or more categories, code in what you determine to be the main topic category.

CODING WRITING PROCESS

Perseverance

DEFINITION: Code as perseverance any topical chain related to an animal's contribution to a writer's ability to persist at writing. This includes references to

    a. an animal's contribution to writing continuance

    b. animal distractions that support or impede perseverance

Disposition

DEFINITION: Code as disposition any topical chain that addresses a frame of mind or feeling related to writing, state of bodily or mental health related to writing, and/or expression of capacity for writing. This includes references to

a. feelings related to writing, e.g., frustration, worry, happiness
b. animal impact on emotional, mental, or physical health
c. motivation and confidence in relation to writing

Proximity

DEFINITION: Code as proximity any topical chain that addresses the condition of animals and writers being near or close by one another in space without reference to feelings or emotional states. This includes references to

a. animals near or on a person as s/he writes
b. spaces where animal and writer cohabitate
c. humans touching animals while writing
d. making eye contact with animals while writing
e. being with or looking at animals in the outdoors during writing breaks

Coding Communication

Modality

DEFINITION: Code as modality any topical chain that addresses a method of communication between human and animal. This includes references to

a. tactile activities, e.g., petting, cuddling, touching
b. reading aloud while animal is nearby, e.g., using animal as sounding board while drafting
c. depictions of animal listening to the writer reading work aloud or talking through an idea
d. nonverbal forms of communication that writer depicts as making a difference to writing, e.g., animal provides company that reassures writer, dog cries to go outside

Effects

DEFINITION: Code as effects any topical chain that addresses the results of communication between humans and animals relative to writing. This includes references to

a. altered affective, mental, or physical states
b. renewed or depleted energy for writing
c. altered perspective on writing

Coding Identity

Self-Perception

DEFINITION: Code as self-perception any topical chain that addresses how contact with animals affects a writer's sense of self. This includes references to

    a. a writer's efficacy, or belief in her/his capacity to succeed as a writer

    b. confidence in one's ability to produce writing

    c. affirmation of value as a person and/or writer

Affect

DEFINITION: Code as affect any topical chain that addresses feelings and/or emotional issues related to animals and composing. This includes references to

    a. emotional support that animals contribute the experience of writing

    b. caring for animals as a valuable emotional experience that positively or negatively influences writing